AXES

AXES

Willa Cather and
William Faulkner

MERRILL MAGUIRE SKAGGS

University of Nebraska Press : Lincoln and London

Library of Congress
Cataloging-in-Publication Data
Skaggs, Merrill Maguire.
  Axes: Willa Cather and William
Faulkner / Merrill Maguire Skaggs.
    p. cm.
Includes bibliographical references
and index.
  ISBN 978-0-8032-1123-0 (cloth:
alk. paper)
1. Cather, Willa, 1873–1947—
Criticism and interpretation.
2. Faulkner, William, 1897–1962—
Criticism and interpretation.
3. Cather, Willa, 1873–1947—
Friends and associates.   4. Faulkner,
William, 1897–1962—Friends and
associates.   5. Cather, Willa, 1873–
1947—Influence.   6. Faulkner,
William, 1897–1962—Influence.
7. Allusions in literature.   I. Title.
  PS3505.A87Z853 2007
  813'.52—dc22   2007010471

Set in Minion and Modula Serif
display by Kim Essman.
Designed by A. Shahan.

*For Marilyn Callander
and Genevieve Owens,
my traveling friends*

CONTENTS

ACKNOWLEDGMENTS

Parts of this book have appeared in earlier versions in my following essays:

"Thefts and Conversation: Cather and Faulkner," reprinted from Cather Studies, vol. 3, ed. Susan J. Rosowski, by permission of the University of Nebraska Press. © 1996 by the University of Nebraska Press.

"Willa Cather's Death Comes for the Archbishop and William Faulkner's The Sound and the Fury," from The Faulkner Journal 13, nos. 1–2 (Fall 1997 / Spring 1998) 89–99. © 1997 and 1998 by the University of Central Florida. Reprinted with permission.

"Willa Cather," in A William Faulkner Encyclopedia, ed. Robert Hamblin and Charles A. Peek, 62–65. Copyright 1999 by Greenwood Press. Reproduced with permission of Greenwood Publishing Group, Inc., Westport CT.

"Willa Cather's Great Emersonian Environmental Quartet," reprinted from Cather Studies, vol. 5, ed. Susan J. Rosowski, by permission of the University of Nebraska Press. © 2003 by the University of Nebraska Press.

"Cather's War and Faulkner's Peace: A Comparison of Two Novels, and More," in Faulkner and His Contemporaries, ed. Joseph R. Urgo and Ann J. Abadie (Jackson: University of Mississippi Press, 2004), 40–53. Used with permission.

INTRODUCTION

THE TITLE OF THIS BOOK originates in Joseph R. Urgo's assertion that Willa Cather and William Faulkner represent "the horizontal and vertical axes of American literature."[1] According to Urgo, Cather's work conveys horizontal movement in space, over a changing landscape, while Faulkner suggests vertical movement in time, or a historical rootedness, especially movement emerging from, then flowing backward into, past time. Urgo's figure of opposite measuring lines seems to me splendidly helpful as a metaphor. I start by applauding it and end, after our writers show they can play each other's side of the board, by reassigning it. I believe the two authors eventually and deliberately change not only their positions but their methods, having carefully assessed each other's life and work. That final gesture to the other may have started as a wave of the fingers with the thumb to the nose, but it ended as a salute and bow. Each writer could play the other's game and each proves it by doing so. And each ends a lifetime's work with an homage to the other.

The purpose of this book is to explain that considered, deliberate set of authorial gestures. To accommodate this volume's *design* (a word sacred to both writers and to such shared mentors as Edgar Allan Poe, Ralph Waldo Emerson, Mark Twain, and Henry James), however, I confess immediately that my title is meant to embrace other meanings. It includes those axes used by miners to dig into pay dirt, *pickaxes*. Faulkner and Cather both poached on and mined each other's claims, in an aggressively predatory way, each digging into the other's staked-out ground with muscular vigor. Further, I acknowledge here the axes of jousters willing to annihilate opponents, *battle-axes*. By 1932 at the latest, Willa and William seem to be charging at each other, while swinging with hopes of landing haymakers. Eventually, both steadied and surveyed their battleground with apparent satisfaction. I think they grew to be proud of each other, even to depend on each other to "get it." The title even embraces the double ax or labrys of Crete, the divine sign of concomitant private and public power, two blades joined in one symbol of completeness. To tell this story about two-steps and fox-trots, contrapuntal maneuvers, feints, fictions, absorptions, assaults, and salutes requires this book.

This story is about many texts in dialogue, written over two productive lifetimes. It's about the lifelong competition between titanic literary ambitions; and it's about mutual literary influence. We will enter here an intricate labyrinth, holding tight to a thread. It will require closest textual readings, some speculative sleuthing, and a willingness to trust the outcome at least long enough for the plot to thicken. Yet before we trace our reversible patterns in the carpet visible beneath two literary careers, we must establish the verifiable facts about this relationship. The facts are skimpy.

Most students know that school dropout William Faulkner trained himself to become a writer by reading. He explained, "When I was young I was an omnivorous reader with no judgment, no discretion—I read everything" (Fant and Ashley 114). Critic Martin Kreiswirth says of Faulkner's method in his early work, "This fundamental derivativeness, far from being accidental or deceitful, represents an attempt on Faulkner's part to follow through a deliberate program of apprenticeship involving discipleship, imitation, and even a kind of outright duplication that approaches plagiarism" (4). Judith Sensibar summarizes, "At twenty-two, Faulkner had read the major novelists of the past three centuries, as well as Shakespeare, the Romantics, the Symbolists, Swinburne, the Georgians, Yeats, and finally, Eliot, Aiken, and other Modernists" (8). One of those modernists was Willa Cather.

A less-often-recognized point is that schooled Willa Cather, while having it out with the Nebraska prairie in her formative adolescent years, followed the same procedure as Faulkner did, with many of the same models and same results. A high school teacher of Cather's once remarked, "She needs to brush up with people who know a lot more than she does" (Kvasnicka 64). Instead, she found most of her superiors in books. So she too practiced omnivorous reading, which included contemporaries, romantics, and eventually modernists.[2] As an adult in New York, she knew Mark Twain personally, as well as other iconoclasts living around her Bank Street apartment near Washington Square.[3] Both of our writers are essentially self-schooled, as geniuses are likely to be; both read everything all the time, as lifelong habits. And both reshaped and recycled in their work what they read and saw. Once they focused on each other, they would read quickly, see penetratingly, and assimilate with confidence.

Faulkner never made any bones about what he did with all those writers he read: "A writer is completely rapacious, he has no morals whatever, he will steal from any source. He's so busy stealing and using it that he himself probably never knows where he gets what he uses. . . . He is influenced by every word he ever read, I think, every sound he ever heard, every sense he ever experienced: and he is so busy writing that he hasn't time to stop and say, 'Now where did I steal this from?' But he did steal it somewhere" (*Lion* 128). Cather made the same practice sound more polite: "I paid Miss Hall the highest compliment one writer can pay another; I stole from her" (*Willa Cather on Writing* 65). An important point, however, is that both these confessions were made when the writers were feeling secure about their reputations. Cather's concession that she stole from Gertrude Hall's book on Wagnerian opera also deflected attention to "critical" or musical sources of her allusions. She was silent here about other "creative" writers, though she elsewhere disingenuously dismissed her imitativeness—or allusive propensities—to Henry James and Edith Wharton.[4] Her preface to Hall's *Wagnerian Romances* was printed first in 1925, by which time she'd long been reiving from both biographical and fictional life stories, as well as from all genres of creative and performing arts. She left the Gertrude Hall preface to be reprinted in her posthumous *On Writing* of 1949, a very premeditated volume.

It remains to establish how often our two writers explicitly acknowledged each other. We may be dealing with the two most secretive writers of the twentieth century here. Cather, of course, tried to mandate that all her letters be burned. They weren't, but they also haven't been collected and published. The best compendium, compromised by Cather's prohibition against direct quotation, and out-of-date as soon as issued because Cather letters destined for archives are now turning up in almost every season, is Janis P. Stout's *A Calendar of the Letters of Willa Cather*. It is composed of summaries and contains no references to Faulkner. Cather had a firm rule against commenting publicly on any living writers. That makes very singular the fact that she mentions both Faulkner and D. H. Lawrence in an addendum attached to her essay "148 Charles Street," ostensibly a loving recollection of Annie Fields, which she collected—as I will show later, not at all carelessly with its addendum attached—in *Not Under Forty*. The addendum allows her to stress the publication date of the reference—1936—fourteen years after she published the essay proper. The fact will eventually, I hope, prove arresting.

Faulkner acknowledged Cather at intervals throughout his career, early, middle, and late.[5] He wrote Anita Loos in a letter he dated "Something Febry 1926": "I am still rather Victorian in my prejudices regarding the intelligence of women, despite Elinor Wylie and Willa Cather and all the balance of them" (*Selected Letters* 32). When prodded in 1948 to name significant contemporary writers, at the University of Mississippi in the year following her death, Faulkner first put Cather in the top five and then substituted his own name for hers (*Lion* 55). This ambiguous gesture could mean that he considered her his only real rival. In any case, when University of Virginia students asked in 1957 whether he read women writers, he immediately cited Brontë, Willa Cather, and Ellen Glasgow (Gwynn and Blotner 202). By the time the State Department had sent him abroad to Japan as a Nobel-winning cultural ambassador, Faulkner was using Cather as a kind of literary bridge-across-the-waters: "There are some works of several people which are first rate. I can name the ones that I was impressed with and that probably influenced me to an extent that I still like to read—one a woman, Willa Cather—I think she is known in Japan" (*Lion* 167–68). The point for us, then, is that both these startlingly private, elusive, secretive, and evasive writers made a point to salute each other publicly. Each must have been aware of the other, and of the implications of the salute, for a long time.

This fact has been hard on their admirers. The devotees, as the writers, do seem opposite each other in every way. Thus, readers who gravitate eagerly toward one writer sometimes stagger repelled from the other. Each writer has battalions of defenders and supporters, not to mention scholars whose egos can seem to be at stake in questions about how writers are ranked. What I will argue here is that the two writers had their eyes on the prize, and therefore on each other, steadily, after 1921. Each measured the other unblinkingly and found a worthy peer. Both writers were profoundly proud, competitive, and ambitious. Each aspired to be America's greatest. Not surprisingly, then, they seem to have infuriated each other after a while, and to have made sure the other knew it. That initial back-and-forthing phased into killer ping-pong before the contest cooled. But add the eventual scores we will tally here however we will, both ended their careers saluting the other, as well as revising the other and one-upping the other, while insistently rewriting the other. By the end they seem almost to have invented the other, if only by constant goading. I think no other literary relationship was ever so surreptitious, so enduring, so intense, or so profoundly productive. We readers are its lucky heirs.

AA: *Absalom, Absalom!*

AILD: *As I Lay Dying*

ALL: *A Lost Lady*

Blotner: one-volume condensed biography of Faulkner

Blotner 1 or 2: biography of Faulkner in two volumes

CCC: Caspersen Cather Collection (Drew University)

DCA: *Death Comes for the Archbishop*

GDM: *Go Down, Moses*

KA: *The Kingdom of Art*

LA: *Light in August*

Lark: *The Song of the Lark*

LG: *Lucy Gayheart*

Lion: *Lion in the Garden: Interviews with William Faulkner, 1926–1962*

M: *Mosquitoes*

MA: *My Ántonia*

MF: *The Marble Faun*

NR: "Neighbour Rosicky"

NUF: *Not Under Forty*

OB: *The Old Beauty and Others*

OMH: "Old Mrs. Harris"

OO: *One of Ours*

PH: *The Professor's House*

SF: *The Sound and the Fury*

SP: *Soldiers' Pay*

SPOW: *[Cather's] Stories, Poems and Other Works*

SSG: *Sapphira and the Slave Girl*

TF: "Two Friends"

TOS: "Tom Outland's Story"

WCPMN&R: *Willa Cather Pioneer Memorial Newsletter and Review*

AXES

1

A Starting Point

IN 1921 WILLIAM FAULKNER had been educating himself by reading omnivorously for about two years, starting or gathering speed after he was mustered out of the RAF in December 1918. He had determined to be not only a writer but also a great writer, and had started by writing poetry to his lost love Estelle. As David Minter summarizes the period, "By 1919 writing had already become the last phase in an educational process so acquisitive as to seem imperial. It was as though nothing he read truly belonged to him until he had echoed, imitated, or adapted it" (36). Eventually, to escape the hometown where he seemed an all-round failure, he had come to live in Greenwich Village, in New York, and to work in Doubleday's Bookstore. The war, which ended before he could participate in it, much less distinguish himself in it, still lay heavy on his mind, and he created fictions about himself and his war activities that he steadily embellished.

In 1921 Willa Cather also had the war on her mind, and was about to accomplish a lifelong ambition. It had been delayed by four years of anxiety about such an enormous task; but as early as 1895 she had declared in print, "When a woman writes a story of adventure, a stout sea tale, a manly battle yarn, anything without wine, women, and love, then I will begin to hope for something great from them, not before" (KA, Nov. 23, 1895). She was preparing the manly battle yarn with stout sea tale incorporated, which would justify her intended achievements. About to meet her own challenge to women, she had been obsessively checking and polishing her facts as she finished her manuscript. She had borrowed a doctor's shipboard diary to verify her account of decimated troops trapped on the Atlantic in an influenza epidemic. She had based her character of David Gerhardt on a real concert violinist. She had checked and rechecked the biographical facts about her cousin G. P. Cather's life, for he was the fallen soldier who was to model her protagonist, the prototypical one-of-ours. This obsessive need of the 1921 late summer moment, to know *exactly* what had happened in the brains of those men who had served in the armed forces, can explain why Cather's cool eyes would focus, then rest, on Bill Faulkner, should he cross her line of vision.

The harder question initially is *not* why Faulkner would find Cather compelling. She was already a celebrity writer whose last novel, *My Ántonia*, had been lavishly praised by H. L. Mencken in *Smart Set* (Woodress 300). The initial stumper is why William Faulkner, once he set out to write a great war novel, would use Willa Cather as a model to imitate, when he could choose from half the world's male storytellers to mentor him in writing about fighters. That question triggers this volume. Yet, as this chapter will show, that's what he seems to have done.

To ask the harder question, I must begin where my own questions first started. Reading *One of Ours* for the first time years ago, I spotted an affinity so unexpected and unsettling that it made me gasp. It happened when I was about halfway through Cather's Pulitzer Prize–winning war novel. Suddenly on the page before me—like an infamous, awful print-shop error—was a passage that looked to me like signature Faulkner. It described mules, and especially reminded me of the "great mule trope" in *Sartoris* (278–79), Faulkner's third novel, his first Yoknapatawpha volume, published in 1929. *Sartoris* is also the saga of that supposedly part-autobiographical clan characterized by "pride, false pride" (*Sartoris* 74). Cather's passage reads like this:

> But wasn't it just like him to be dragged into matrimony by a pair of mules!
>
> He laughed as he looked at them. "You old devils, you're strong enough to play such tricks on green fellows for years to come. You're chock full of meanness!"
>
> One of the animals wagged an ear and cleared his throat threateningly.
>
> Mules are capable of strong affections, but they hate snobs, are the enemies of caste, and this pair had always seemed to detect in Claude what his father used to call his "false pride." When he was a young lad they had been a source of humiliation to him, braying and balking in public places, trying to show off at the lumber yard or in front of the postoffice. (OO 215)

Since the language and vocabulary here is appropriate to the character thinking these thoughts, I could reassure myself that Cather must have controlled the recording pencil. But the sardonic brain and the malevolent mules seemed so Faulknerian that I rechecked the facts. Sure enough, Cather's novel appeared in 1922, when Faulkner had published outside Mississippi only one poem in the *New Republic*, and "L'Après-Midi d'un Faune" didn't sound mulish.

A plausible conclusion seemed to be that Willa had beaten William to the typesetter in mentioning mulish barnyard tricks. I was shaken, however, by these then-forbidden thoughts: Cather had a Faulkneresque streak; and Faulkner might have learned a trick or two from her. I read on with eyes alert for other signs. Thus, I was awake when in the last section of Cather's novel, set in wartime France, I spotted the central figure and controlling plot device of Faulkner's first novel, *Soldier's Pay* (1926).

The character of the maimed American amnesiac soldier, whom women love and experts find worth recording, is described this way by a doctor in Cather's French military hospital:

"Oh, yes! He's a star patient here, a psychopathic case. I had just been talking to one of the doctors about him, when I came out and saw you with him. He was shot in the neck at Cantigny, where he lost his arm. The wound healed, but his memory is affected; some nerve cut, I suppose, that connects with that part of his brain. This psychopath, Phillips, takes a great interest in him and keeps him here to observe him. He's writing a book about him. He says the fellow has forgotten almost everything about his life before he came to France. The queer thing is, it's his recollection of women that is most affected. He can remember his father, but not his mother; doesn't know if he has sisters or not,—can remember seeing girls about the house, but thinks they may have been cousins. His photographs and belongings were lost when he was hurt, all except a bunch of letters he had in his pocket. They are from a girl he's engaged to, and he declares he can't remember her at all: doesn't know what she looks like or anything about her, and can't remember getting engaged. The doctor has the letters. They seem to be from a nice girl in his own town who is very ambitious for him to make the most of himself. He deserted soon after he was sent to this hospital, ran away. He was found on a farm out in the country here, where the sons had been killed and the people had sort of adopted him. He'd probably have got away with it, if he hadn't had that wry neck. Some one saw him in the fields and recognized him and reported him. I guess nobody cared much but this psychopathic doctor; he wanted to get his pet patient back. They call him 'the lost American' here." (287)

Faulkner likely found a number of details in this passage useful when he constructed his collage of a lost generation. They include the soldier's terrible scarring or wounding; a hand he has lost use of; his amnesia, which especially covers women, sweethearts, and fiancée; his lost papers as well as a recovered letter from the girl back home; his good family background; his engagement to a "nice" girl who wants him to shine in the community; concerned helpers who surround him; and most especially, his centrality to an unpublished book. Faulkner's lost American, symbolically named Lieutenant Donald Mahon, suggests to me both a representative man (Mahon in a Southern drawl) and a dead duck (Donald). Cather's protagonist, equally symbolic, is Lieutenant Claude (clawed) Wheeler, who experiences war as euphoria until the wheel of fortune spins him round. Claude gets a war that he loves in spite of his "chump" (oo 17) and "sissy" (oo 279) first name, which his wife pronounces *clod*. Faulkner incorporates the name *Claude* into *Soldier's Pay* as the generic name of a railroad porter (*sp* 24). The second novel Faulkner planned but never completed played on the same kind of chump name: *Elmer*.

A foretaste of reversals to come, Faulkner's novel takes up where Cather's leaves off—soldiers returning from the war. That extension helps obscure dozens of interesting overlaps in these works, the first, the symbolic use of a train as a linear vehicle paradoxically suggesting life's circularity. Cather had first used this device in *My Ántonia* to start her novel twice, and eventually used either doubled beginnings or endings (or both) in *Death Comes for the Archbishop*, *Shadows on the Rock*, and *Sapphira and the Slave Girl*. These last three novels, all as yet unwritten in 1921, especially held the attention of that careful reader William Faulkner. *One of Ours*, however, illustrates the usefulness of this doubling device when Cather must show something two ways in the middle of her book. Claude's war starts first when he has a last leave before shipping overseas. He goes home on the train, proves himself responsible on home ground by halting the hooligan harassment of a good German lunch-counter cook, and then is given a hero's welcome by his family and neighbors who had previously joked about him. Later, literally off to war at last, he successfully controls his men on a troop train stalled near Hoboken docks. On both trains he is in transition, but moving irrevocably toward his fate, as well as toward the increasingly outstanding military leadership of which he is capable. Thus, by Faulknerian standards, he deserves his hero's death as well as his opportunity to enjoy a hero's glory first, before dying.

Faulkner reverses this train journey to bring his soldier home at his beginning, and to take the maternal Margaret Powers away at his conclusion. But he signals the use of reversals under the camouflaging white noise through which these two writers will hold their conversations in public, while their personally challenging words remain inaudible except to each other. Obviously many writers use trains to move characters along. Readers tend to pay little attention to cars moving on tracks. But each of our writers notices how others move people along physically and psychologically. To use a device a new way, all they have to do is invert, reverse, or turn inside out some centrally dominant thing or fact—like the direction of a train. I believe that's how they carried on their unnoticed and prolonged turnabout literary steal-the-flag games.

When Cather's Claude Wheeler returns home by train briefly before shipping out, he recognizes the anti-German violence rife in the American Midwest; in moving by train toward his tall ship, he discovers the frustrating delays of troop movements. And when Faulkner's soldiers start home on a train, the scene is even more frustrating and chaotic; his men are drunk and disorderly. But they, too, are in significant transit, already hopelessly trying to circle back to home places into which they cannot fit—a humiliation Claude Wheeler is explicitly spared. Faulkner deals with the soldier's return, while Claude dies suddenly, believing in the delusion that life had turned out well for him (oo 349). All this jerky transportation dramatizes the opposite of easy riding, and in it, one sees destinies. Faulkner's one caring woman rolls away down the track, and leaves helpless men behind. Cather's ending leaves Wheeler's men at sea, while a dimwitted Wheeler housemaid prays naively in the last sentence to a God she believes hovers just above her kitchen stove. So in each war novel, a caring woman is present at the end, but does not count significantly in future lives of male characters.

Before discussing significantly similar themes developed in these two novels, I'd like to salute Faulkner's shrewd eye and swift assimilation of useable material, whenever he read Willa Cather. While *Soldier's Pay* can actually be considered an *homage* to several Cather novels—including *My Ántonia, A Lost Lady,* and *The Professor's House*—the observing eye that pays homage is auspicious. *To reive* or steal is a verb he not only ended his career underscoring; he also uses it three times as he begins his novelist's career with *Soldier's Pay* (SP 58, 70, 291). His thefts are quality reiving. They must have impressed Willa Cather, for she contrived her unprecedented tribute to a living author, written in contradiction of her own expressed principle,[1] by quoting an eponymous schoolboy who writes from his educational trenches, "D. H. Lawrence is rather rated a back-number here, but Faulkner keeps his end up" (NUF 74). Obviously, Faulkner is not the only one in this odd couple who has a good eye, a sharp pencil, and a propensity for deadpan punning. Further, both writers show a willingness to disrupt the "unities" in fictions about World War I, thus sharing a technique. Both see that disruption is fitting when one is writing about carnage. In both fictions settings dissolve, names change, characters suddenly appear and disappear, platitudes are contradicted by experience, and all strings are not tied. Judging from an Aristotelian point of view, both writers acknowledge that fiction about war is hell.

One very startling similarity between the two, however, is their agreement that war itself can be heaven, even preferable to peace, if peace is too static to bear. On his rich Nebraska farm Cather's

Claude Wheeler feels "weak and broken" (134), promises to become "one of those dead people that moved about the streets" (179), recognizes another description of life as "a sleeping sickness" (262), and "didn't find this kind of life worth the trouble of getting up every morning" (89). He feels "driven into the ground like a post, or like those Chinese criminals who are planted upright in the earth, with only their heads left out for birds to peck at and insects to sting" (243). His Nebraska is so dull that even the theatrical events are *tableaux vivants*—living pictures in which the players freeze (108). Everything about the drama of war seems better to him than Nebraska. This *everything* includes Claude's responsibility to care for his men as influenza carries them away, or his repeated risk of his life in France, or even his final dramatic dismemberment by a German land mine: all better. Since he's from Frankfort, a German-sounding Nebraska hometown, the war is almost like home, only a lot happier and more interesting. In fact, he's most at home when at war. Or, perhaps, the enemy is home. Like a Sartoris man, who feels when at home like "a trapped beast" (*Sartoris* 203), Claude, like Sartorises, seems to think of war as "a holiday" (*Sartoris* 10).

Faulkner recognizes in *Soldier's Pay* that Cather has earned the Pulitzer by fictionalizing these suspicions. He repeats them. "We heard you was dead, or in the piano business or something," one of Faulkner's returning soldiers says impertinently to a civilian (*SP* 16). Faulkner's Cadet Julian Lowe feels overpowering envy when he considers that grotesquely scarred Lieutenant Mahon is going blind as he lies dying: "How the man managed to circumvent him at every turn! As if it were not enough to have wings and a scar. But to die!" For "what was death to Cadet Lowe, except something true and grand and sad. . . . What more could one ask of Fate?" (*SP* 52). Both novels patronize this romantic peevishness. Within her novel, however, Cather uses three of her five "books" to explain how such love of war can possibly exist; Faulkner just starts by assuming it.

Both novelists ask a reader to remember that this view of war is supposed to be a "blockhead" view. Claude is identified as a blockhead quickly (oo 17), and Cather stresses the word: "He especially hated his head—so big that he had trouble in buying his hats, and uncompromisingly square in shape; a perfect block-head." Ironically, the insulting German epithet *boche* also means *blockhead*. According to Webster's *New World Dictionary* of 1960, *boche* in 1865 French slang is short for *caboche*, hardhead. It was next found in printer's argot as *tête carée (d'Allemand)*, or literally, the square head (of a German). Later shortened to *boche*, the term is always hostile. Again, the enemy blockheads we fight hardest may be ourselves, may live in our own homes—or heads.

Blockhead or not, the love of war comes first in the hearts of these American country men. Faulkner's drunken dischargees label America the foreign country and add, "Listen, think of having to go to work again when you get home. Ain't war hell? I would have been a corporal at least, if she had just hung on another year" (*SP* 10). The train conductor can see, "My God.... If we ever have another peace I don't know what the railroads will do. I thought war was bad, but my God" (*SP* 12).

Somehow these Faulkner lines fail to surprise. What surprises is that Cather tells the same story first. Hearing of the slaughter along the Marne, Claude knows "he was not the only farmer boy who wished himself tonight beside the Marne" (oo 148). Knowing the danger, he also knows that "there was nothing on earth he would so gladly be as an atom in that wall of flesh and blood" (oo 149). Once he gets on board ship and away from home, Claude thinks, "In this massing and movement of men there was nothing mean or common, he was sure of that" (243). Once in uniform, he knows who he is, what he should do with his life, and what happiness feels like. Like most of his men, he's eager to get into action as soon as possible, and thinks of the front as "the big show" (305). That's the surprise—how much Cather's Claude loves war, and how much William Faulkner chooses to believe other soldiers do, too.

Cather spends 60 percent of her novel explaining why Claude is a discontented, poorly educated, frustrated, bitter young man who doesn't enjoy farmwork. He is eager to escape the farm and see some action in France. No wonder basically *un*original Claude is so proud of what he's doing, and so ready to believe "it was worth having lived in this world to have known such men" (*oo* 303). War is his vocation, his calling, and he responds to it with religious zeal and zest. As a veteran, Faulkner does not quarrel with any part of Cather's picture. He quarrels with history for leaving him out of the fight.

In both novels, however, a commonsense explanation for the way these soldiers got—or get—so unhappy at home seems to be the women. Cather's Enid, the competent home manager who was meant for business or the missionary life, but whose very father warns that she is not designed for a wife, is the model for the disappointing women. Enid does all her housework dressed in white—like a professional nurse in an institution for the infirm. Claude thinks of marrying her after his mules have run him into a barbed-wire fence and he has developed erysipelas. Once he's immobilized in bandages, Enid comes unselfconsciously into his bedroom to cheer him up by playing chess. Similarly, in *Sartoris*, Narcissa Benbow comes into young Bayard's sickroom to read to him, once his chest is crushed. As Claude does, Bayard thereafter marries this inappropriate bride, while Narcissa speaks of Bayard as "the beast, the beast" (155). The attitude of Cather's Enid is explained succinctly: "Everything about a man's embrace was distasteful to Enid; something inflicted upon women, like the pain of childbirth,—for Eve's transgression, perhaps" (180).

What is interesting is the extent to which Faulkner accepts Enid as his coverall prototype. His dislike for the hometown flirt Cecily Saunders, Mahon's forgotten fiancée, is unremitting; she is never described positively. Mrs. Powers, his young war widow who chooses to use her husband's life insurance to finance her taking care of totally needy Mahon, would seem to be different. Yet Margaret Powers, who hardly remembers her husband, thinks, "How ugly men are, naked" (*SP* 182), and mutters repeatedly when he crosses her mind, "Dear, ugly, dead Dick" (184). She asks, "Am I cold by nature, or have I spent all my emotional coppers, that I don't seem to feel things like others? Dick, Dick. Ugly and dead" (39). Mrs. Powers marries Mahon as an act of charity when he is nearly dead and already blind, and after all the other females she has proposed sacrificial marriage to, have refused it. After Mahon dies, she refuses to marry the devoted Joe Gilligan, who acts as Mahon's body servant and orderly, because she just can't tolerate his name. In Cather's liberated Beaufort, French women show an American squadron a good time, but that's after they've been locked away from occupying Germans, and without men, for four stressful years. Mostly, in both novels mother love is the best a man ever gets, and that's basically what Mrs. Powers offers Donald Mahon. Making the same point, the most passionate kiss in *One of Ours* is between Claude and his mother (225).

Perhaps one reason Willa Cather and William Faulkner have sounded discordant, when put in the same sentence, has to do with Faulkner's abundant and mordant humor, and the assumption that Cather doesn't have any. Without leaping outside her war novel for barricades from which to fight this tone-deaf opinion, I'd suggest that *One of Ours* has plenty of humor, though I grant that most of it develops at Claude's expense. Thus, readers who identify with Claude may fail to be amused. For example, when Claude and Sergeant Hicks are returning from field headquarters to their squad at the front, they hear of a shortcut they may use once night falls. They take their daylight time getting to it, and Cather's story proceeds:

When they struck the road they came upon a big Highlander sitting in the end of an empty supply wagon, smoking a pipe and rubbing the dried mud out of his kilts. . . . The Americans hadn't happened to meet with any Highlanders before. . . . This one must be a good fighter, they thought; a brawny giant with a bulldog jaw, and a face as red and knobby as his knees. More because he admired the looks of the man than because he needed information, Hicks went up and asked him if he had noticed a military cemetery on the road back. The kiltie nodded.

"About how far back would you say it was?"

"I wouldn't say at all. I take no account of their kilometers," he said drily, rubbing away at his skirt as if he had it in a washtub.

"Well, about how long will it take us to walk it?"

"That I couldn't say. A Scotsman would do it in an hour."

"I guess a Yankee can do it as quick as a Scotchman, can't he?" Hicks asked jovially.

"That I couldn't say. You've been four years gettin' this far, I know verra well."

Hicks blinked as if he had been hit. "Oh, if that's the way you talk—"

"That's the way I do," said the other sourly.

Claude put out a warning hand. "Come on, Hicks. You'll get nothing by it."

They went up the road very much disconcerted. Hicks kept thinking of things he might have said. (oo 334–35)

While speed-readers can also associate Cather with blandness, she models in *One of Ours* literary horror as well as humor. The worst horror in both these novels occurs in a trench. When Claude's men first occupy trenches the Germans have just vacated, they must deal not only with gunfire ahead and shells bursting nearby. They must also man guns placed amid inadequately buried German bodies. First a black hand keeps reappearing with its fingers splayed out as if grabbing or beckoning them. Then a boot reappears, though they repeatedly try to bury these body parts. Reappearing dead limbs are chilling portents of what will soon happen to the Americans. The trench has been mined by retreating Germans whose preplanned return will start by blowing Americans apart.

A strong link between the two novels, however, is the association of the trenches with lethal gas attacks. In Faulkner's riff, when Mahon's local squadmates were green recruits, they were sent to such a trench, led by Margaret Powers's bridegroom, Richard. Mistakenly deducing that Richard has led them to sure death by gas, one soldier shoots him in the face as he approaches with words of cheer.

No matter how many dozens of similar details, themes, and characters one compiles between these two books, however—and there are many to compare—they do not sufficiently explain the singular grip of *One of Ours* on unpublished Bill Faulkner's imagination. So now we take a look at a very bizarre coincidence. In the middle of Cather's novel is a character who matches the real Bill Faulkner as he was presenting himself inventively *at this time*. We can recognize him because we've seen his photograph (Blotner 1:200), nattily dressed in his RAF uniform, sporting a cane, and reportedly posing as a walking war-wounded. As Blotner describes Faulkner during a short interval in the crucial late summer and early autumn of 1921 (when Cather was back on Bank Street and polishing *One of Ours*), he was living in Greenwich Village, in closest proximity to Washington Square. At this time, Blotner tells us, Faulkner tended to drop in at dinnertime on a couple called the Joices. Mrs. Joice recalls,

> "He was just back from the war and, in fact, he had a cane and walked with a limp. He was dressed in a light beige mackintosh, a dusty dark brown hat and a pipe. He was generally nice

looking with dark brown eyes[2] and hair. . . . He did nothing to dispel my illusion that he was a wounded hero returning from France." [When he finally removed the macintosh] he wore a drab gray suit which gave off an odor she took to be a combination of alcohol and perspiration. [Yet he was] "so mystique" that her interest cooled [only] when he asked . . . for a loan until he received some money from home, which was "a Southern plantation." (Blotner 1:324)

Blotner summarizes, "The persona of the wounded pilot had made another appearance, as it would sometimes do when Faulkner found himself in a new environment. He had created an impression partly through his fictitious story and partly through assumptions he allowed his hearers to make" (1:324–25). After Faulkner returned to the South, Blotner quotes from James K. Feibleman's description of him in New Orleans that winter as "a little man with a well-shaped head, a small moustache and a slightly receding chin," who held himself aloof and apart until he had something he wanted to say, such as, "I could write a play like *Hamlet* if I wanted to" (1:330).

Now visualize the character in *One of Ours* whom Cather names Victor Morse—a code name for a hero, if there ever was one. Cather's physical description matches the Bill Faulkner who wrote home about learning Morse code during his aeronautical training (Blotner 1:213). She also captures his evolving tall tales. Victor Morse climbs aboard Claude Wheeler's ship in *One of Ours*, having come straight by taxi from New York's St. Regis Hotel:

When Claude and Fanning and Lieutenant Bird were undressing in their narrow quarters that night, the fourth berth was still unclaimed. They were in their bunks and almost asleep, when the missing man came in and unceremoniously turned on the light. They were astonished to see that he wore the uniform of the Royal Flying Corps and carried a cane. He seemed very young, but the three who peeped out at him felt that he must be a person of consequence. He took off his coat with the spread wings on the collar, wound his watch, and brushed his teeth with an air of special personal importance. Soon after he had turned out the light and climbed into the berth over Lieutenant Bird, a heavy smell of rum spread in the close air. (236–37)

Throughout the next day, reports reach Claude about their new cabinmate. Finally, he can stand the suspense no longer.

Claude was curious, and went down to the cabin. As he entered, the air-man, lying half-dressed in his upper berth, raised himself on one elbow and looked down at him. His blue eyes were contracted and hard, his curly hair disordered, but his cheeks were as pink as a girl's, and the little yellow humming-bird mustache on his upper lip was twisted sharp. . . .

He drew a bottle from under his pillow. "Have a nip?"

"I don't mind if I do," Claude put out his hand.

The other laughed and sank back on his pillow, drawling lazily, "Brave boy! Go ahead, drink to the Kaiser."

"Why to him in particular?"

"It's not particular. Drink to Hindenburg, or the High Command, or anything else that got you out of the cornfield. That's where they did get you, didn't they?"

"Well, it's a good guess, anyhow. Where did they get you?"

"Crystal Lake, Iowa. . . ." He yawned and folded his hands over his stomach.

"Why, we thought you were an Englishman."

"Not quite. I've served in His Majesty's army two years, though."

"Have you been flying in France?"

"Yes. I've been back and forth all the time, England and

France. Now I've wasted two months at Forth Worth. Instructor. That's not my line. . . ."

All the same, Claude wanted to find out how a youth from Crystal Lake ever became a member of the Royal Flying Corps. Already, from among the hundreds of strangers, half-a-dozen stood out as men he was determined to know better. (239–40)

I suspect that Victor Morse is from Crystal Lake, Iowa, because Cather thinks she can see straight through him. In any case, soon after this conversation Victor Morse mentions hoping to report to London first: "He continued to gaze off at the painted ships.[3] Claude noticed that in standing he held his chin very high. His eyes, now that he was quite sober, were brilliantly young and daring; they seemed scornful of things about him. He held himself conspicuously apart, as if he were not among his own kind. Claude had seen a captured crane, tied by its leg to a hencoop, behave exactly like that . . . hold its wings to its sides, and move its head about quickly and glare (245)." Soon Morse is telling gullible Claude Wheeler about his London mistress, who has given him a photograph with "Á mon aigle!" — to my eagle — scrawled across it (262). And to this day, anybody in Washington Square or the Northeast who mentions an acquaintance in Oxford will be heard to be talking of England. I, at least, mentioned often in New Jersey in 2002 that I was going to a Faulkner Conference in Oxford. I was repeatedly rumored to be going abroad, or asked how long I'd be overseas.

The most striking fact we must register here is that Willa Cather gives her coded Victor Morse the desired death William Faulkner would most have preferred at this time. He later incorporates it into his fiction. In Cather's novel Claude Wheeler is later told, "Morse the American ace? Hadn't he heard? Why that got into the London papers. Morse was shot down inside the Hun line three weeks ago. It was a brilliant affair. He was chased by eight Boche planes, brought down three of them, put the rest to flight, and was making for base, when they turned and got him. His machine came down in flames and he jumped, fell a thousand feet or more" (oo 318–19). Claude thinks mournfully, "He had really liked Victor. There was something about that fellow . . . a sort of debauched baby, he was, who went seeking his enemy in the clouds. What other age could have produced such a figure? That was one of the things about this war: it took a little fellow from a little town, gave him an air and a swagger, a life like a movie-film, —and then a death like the rebel angels" (319).

Faulkner's third novel, *Sartoris*, matches every detail in this portrait without answering the insistent questions, how much of the portrait is whole-cloth fiction, and if fiction, whose fiction? In Faulkner's version young Bayard Sartoris returns to Memphis in the middle of the war to teach aviators in a flying school (54); he is said to have "knocked two teeth out of an Australian captain that just tried to speak to a girl he was with in a London dive two years ago" (360); he is associated with eagles, through the epitaph on his twin brother John's grave (374) and the Sartoris burial plot that seems "the eyrie of an eagle" (375); he tries to emulate that brother's cocky death like the rebel angels (321); the news of each death is conveyed by a newspaper, and in Johnny's case, "a limey paper" (319) spotted by Buddy MacCallum; and John's jaunty death is reported by Bayard, who at the crucial moment was airborne and trying to protect his brother John from the pursuing Huns (43).

These duplications nudge our answer, I think. Unless we are willing to label Willa Cather as the creator of the earliest Faulkner fictions and the progenitress of the Yoknapatawpha saga, which I am not, then we must suspect that while they were in the same neighborhood of New York's Greenwich Village, in late summer of 1921, William Faulkner may have vividly told his current stories to Willa Cather. She liked what she heard and promptly folded them and him into her new novel. Recognizing himself in her fiction, he thereafter felt free to plunder her work thoroughly, if indeed he needed any such excuse. But he trusted her to give him work worth plundering for two good reasons: one, because she had showed her good taste by liking him first — all of him, the real one as well as the one he conjured, plus the one who told brilliantly the tall tales about a life like the rebel angels, to her satisfaction. The second reason, of course, was that she had showed him how a real writer reives, and he liked the idea.

By relying on James Woodress's biography of Cather we can locate rather precisely the time in which they could have encountered each other. Cather returned to New York from nearly five months' stay with Jan and Isabelle Hambourg, having completed a draft of *One of Ours*, in August of 1921. In the momentary relief, in late August and early September, she could begin to relax after four arduous years' work. She was not only back in New York catching her breath, but also preparing for a long trip back to Nebraska and the homeplaces of G. P. Cather. By early October, she received in Red Cloud a congratulatory telegram from Alfred A. Knopf, who had just received her manuscript, eagerly read her novel, and admired it. Cather, thereafter, was lionized in Nebraska and then made her way home to New York through Chicago. Arriving in the City in early November, she was exhausted enough to go to bed for a week, afflicted with a "misbehaving colon." Soon thereafter she entered a Pennsylvania sanatorium. Thus the only possible "window" for an encounter with William Faulkner seems to have been the last days of August and the first days of early September, when Faulkner, too, was momentarily expansive with the pleasure of a new life in New York City. That's also when the weather usually encourages sauntering slowly down city sidewalks, or resting and people-watching on Washington Square benches (Woodress 318–21). Cather's hypothetical need to incorporate what she saw and heard immediately, if she is to use it at all, in set pieces of Faulkner's performance art and tale-telling conversation, straight from sidewalk to manuscript insertion, tallies with the time lines biographers have established.

Four years later in 1925, Cather was described in an essay by Thomas Beer for an in-house publication called *The Borzoi*, published by Alfred A. Knopf to celebrate his own publishing house. Beer is distressingly clever, but claims in "Miss Cather" to know Cather personally. He takes an arch view of "her stealthy advance in estimation" (24), though it seems less surprising to him because the "decade of Muck, the calamitous ten years from 1900 to 1910, represent the flimsiest period in modern literary history" (24). He observes that her stories such as "A Wagner Matinée" and "The Sculptor's Funeral" counteract Roosevelt's sentimentality about the west. And this, he points out, is a dangerous gambit. But he explains not only that "Miss Cather has had the courage to stroll on eggshells" (27), but also that "She walks a good deal in Washington Square where ashcans are prevalent" (30). Walkers in that City Square can spot each other, share benches and talk, even begin to tell anecdotes and stories. If both are also fine listeners and observers, as both of our writers were said to be, they may even swap narratives for immediate or future use in fiction. These two seem to have done so.

2

Buzzing

SO FAR AS AN EYE can presently see, Willa Cather hardly acknowledged *Soldier's Pay*, with the exception of one nod through
a name mentioned briefly in "Before Breakfast," her last story.
Nor did she exhibit any embarrassment whatsoever, at any time,
about her implanted provocations to William Faulkner in *One of
Ours*. Thus, she, a lifelong advocate of "natural good manners,"
modeled the social habits to shape their exchanges. Faulkner's
second novel, *Mosquitoes* (1927), however, was another matter.
In *Mosquitoes*, Faulkner plundered thoroughly the salient possibilities he chose from Cather's *The Professor's House* (1925). During her *Professor's House* preparation time, she had told an interviewer writing for *The Borzoi* that she had strolled on eggshells
while in Washington Square Park. The comment seems relevant
to Faulkner, as we shall see (Beer 27).

Faulkner wrote *Mosquitoes* in the remainder of 1926, after the
publications of his first and Cather's seventh novel. Years later,
Cather dedicated a good percentage of her last printed story, published posthumously in 1948, to addressing *Mosquitoes*. While we
must delay a thorough look at that astonishing performance till
chapter 9, we have an immediate right to be curious about why
the buzzing of the immature *Mosquitoes* bothered her so much.
Faulkner is still a fledgling writer; why couldn't mature Cather

shrug it off? She seems unable to rest in her grave without commenting on it in particular, and commenting even after a number of more striking provocations that she might choose from by then. Even in *Mosquitoes*, however, the central situation Faulkner develops closely resembles another Cather work, the early short story "Flavia and Her Artists." *Mosquitoes* depicts an extended houseboat party in which the hospitality of a hostess is abused by a group of ungrateful artists.

To explain what riveted Faulkner's attention to *The Professor's House*, into which his pickaxe dug deeply, is a two-chapter business. Initially, we must establish recognizable connections. *The Professor's House* furnished Faulkner characterization, description, symbols, and themes for this, his second novel. The treasures once stored in St. Peter's attic reappear on display in *Mosquitoes*. Most obvious are the professor's dress forms. They condense (Faulkner will later love multiplying more) into *one* marble statue of a headless, armless, legless female torso, which sculptor Gordon, like Professor St. Peter, will not "relinquish." Gordon describes this creation to which he is deeply attached as "my feminine ideal: a virgin with no legs to leave me, no arms to hold me, no head to talk to me" (*m* 26). In turning the perhaps Platonic ideal forms St. Peter needs beside him in order to think and work, into such a sardonic definition of "feminine ideal," Faulkner is at least one of the first to recognize the philosophical origins of St. Peter's sexist outlook. Cather's Napoleon Godfrey St. Peter is the shaper of histories who internalizes and summarizes the dominant institutions of the phallocentric West, especially of America. Faulkner catches on to what St. Peter embodies immediately.

In the novel then quickly produced, Faulkner's character, the niece Patricia, desires Gordon's marble torso because "it's like me" (*m* 24). In turn, this young woman, as well as the marble torso, resembles St. Peter's daughter Kathleen in *The Professor's House*; all three—the statue, the niece, the daughter—boast what

Cather describes as "the slender, undeveloped figure then very much in vogue" (PH 41), which looks like a boy. That is, St. Peter's dress forms, which can replicate the shape of his youngest daughter so that a seamstress can make her clothes, "transmogrify" in Faulkner's novel to the nubile torso that young Patricia immediately recognizes as herself. Toward the end of *Mosquitoes*, the statue is said to be a metaphorical way to lock up a love so "she couldn't leave" (M 269). That is, the statue keeps the female permanently immutable, static—like a Platonic form. Novelist Dawson Fairchild comments to Gordon, "I see . . . that you too have been caught by this modern day fetish of virginity. But you have this advantage over us: yours will remain inviolate without your having to shut your eyes to its goings-on" (M 318). Here Faulkner addresses, in order to elaborate, St. Peter's fancy that his wire lady "was most convincing in her pose as a woman of light behaviour" (PH 19). Loose living is of course not a Cather endorsement, but it is certainly a revealing way to suggest something interesting about the mind of her professor. St. Peter likes to imagine immobilizing an image of light behavior. Gordon immobilizes better, in marble.

The marble torso is as central to *Mosquitoes* as the dress forms are to *The Professor's House*. Cather says of her black form: "Though this figure looked so ample and billowy (as if you might lay your head upon its deep-breathing softness and rest safe forever), if you touched it you suffered a severe shock, no matter how many times you had touched it before. It presented the most unsympathetic surface imaginable. . . . It was a dead, opaque, lumpy solidity, like chunks of putty, or tightly packed sawdust—very disappointing to the tactile sense, yet somehow always fooling you again" (PH 18).

This change from hard putty to cold marble also follows a lead in *The Professor's House* in which Cather privileges sculpture. To be compared to sculpture in her novel, which the dress forms were *not*, is highest praise. Tom Outland discovers on the Blue

Mesa "a little city of stone, asleep. It was still as sculpture—and something like that" (*PH* 201). Tom feels the place is "a sacred spot" (221). St. Peter, too, longs for the "sculptured peaks" of Outland's country (270). Later, Tom feels such joy in his exclusive possession of the sculptured city that his elation is like a religious emotion. That same religious feeling is aroused again by the "white dome against a flashing blue sky" of the Capitol in Washington (225)—another sculptured architectural monument and a reinforced link between patriarchal religious and political expressions. My point is that insightful young William Faulkner picked up from *The Professor's House* a connection between hard white stone, a careful design, personal possession, and a man's sense of transcendence. The result in *Mosquitoes* is a female torso so compellingly expressive of desire that Patricia recognizes herself in it, and wants to touch and possess it herself. The form is so perfect in its way that Gordon, not unlike St. Peter, would rather possess the form than the girl. St. Peter would rather live with his forms in his old house than with his wife in the new.

In *The Professor's House*, an interest in statuary is not confined to buildings and cities. St. Peter's head, "more like a statue's head than a man's" (*PH* 13), resembles "the heads of the warriors on the Parthenon frieze" (71). It appears that in this Cather novel (as opposed to several others), significant heads are male—especially the marble-hard heads; marble torsos (containing no heads but hard hearts), in Faulkner, are female. St. Peter's head is best, according to Kathleen, "between the top of his ear and his crown"—that is, in the brain or analytical organ (13). The association of brains with self-centered males perhaps explains why Cather said privately that she didn't much like this novel and couldn't understand its popularity (Stout, *Calendar*, no. 798).

Appropriating what Cather says about St. Peter extends Faulkner's novel in several directions. Sculptor Gordon has "a hawk face" (*M* 12, 27), to match St. Peter's "hawk nose, hawk eyes" (*PH* 13). St. Peter's "slender hips and springy shoulders of a tireless swimmer" (*PH* 12) sire Patricia's aquatic appearance: she dives like "a white arrow arcing down the sky," while "clad in a suit of her brother's underwear" (*m* 80, 81). She also swims naked, reminding us that "for looks, the fewer clothes . . . [St. Peter] had on, the better" (*ph* 12). When she emerges from the water, "her taut simple body, almost breastless and with the fleeting hips of a boy, was an ecstasy in golden marble" (*m* 82).

Many of Faulkner's characterizing details in *Mosquitoes* pick up details from *The Professor's House*. Gordon, in his third-floor walk-up studio—analogous to St. Peter's third-floor attic—lives in space completed by "a high useless window framing two tired looking stars" (*m* 22)—analogous to the bad attic window that blows shut in St. Peter's old house. Gordon also, like Tom Outland alone in Cliff City, lives "sufficient unto himself in the city of his arrogance, in the marble tower of his loneliness and pride" (153). But in fact, in one of his earliest New Orleans sketches from February of 1925, Faulkner begins, "My life is a house" (*New Orleans Sketches* 7). The fact reminds us that Faulkner may have spotted a prepublication announcement of Cather's *The Professor's House* in *Collier's*. Certainly before the official book publication in the fall, the professor's helmeted head was visible on the cover of *Collier's*, where the novel was serialized that spring.[1] Tom Outland's story appeared there also.

Duplicating Tom Outland's perch and point of view, Faulkner's sculptor Gordon leans "over the edge of the wharf, staring down into the water" and thinks with consciousness streaming, "stars in my hair in my hair and beard i am crowned with stars christ by his own hand an autogethsemane carved darkly out of pure space" (*m* 47–48). He even, strolling a wharf, sees that the "warehouse, the dock, was a formal rectangle without perspective. Flat as cardboard" (47). That is, he registers a world like the one in Outland's stories, where St. Peter says "there were no shadows" (*ph* 123).

Faulkner's "soft blonde" Jenny (55), "her stainless pink-and-whiteness, ineffable, unmarred by any thought at all" (255), is described more derisively than any other female character in

Mosquitoes. But again, without reflecting Cather's ambivalence toward the professorial intelligence assessing her, Jenny replicates the "very fair, pink and gold, —a pale gold" (*PH* 36) pastels of Lillian, St. Peter's wife. Lillian, in turn, more positively suggests the "pink and pale yellow and tan" that Tom first identifies with the sleeping houses in the Cliff City overarching cavern (208). Deliberately distancing from his wife, St. Peter finds Lillian "less intelligent and more sensible than he had [previously] thought her" (*PH* 79), but that assessment is an offshoot of his emotional evasiveness at this moment.

Another female character, Faulkner's painter Dorothy Jameson,[2] seems to be properly characterized by a liking for "blue jewelry . . . and sapphires in dull silver" (*M* 182). We recognize echoes of the "turquoise set in dull silver" that Louie Marsellus, St. Peter's son-in-law, likes to associate with his wife, Rosamond, particularly when we recall that Louie's eyes "were vividly blue, like hot sapphires" (*PH* 43). Cather went out of her way to describe turquoise as "a soft blue stone" (*PH* 120), which might appropriately, unlike hard sapphires, be set in soft silver. She may have been jolted to read that Faulkner's "yacht was a thick jewel swaddled in soft gray wool," was "motionless, swaddled in mist like a fat jewel" (*M* 164). Cather knows her jewels and how to set them, or set them off, as Faulkner learns after his second novel.

The complete list of Catherian items reappearing in Faulkner's *Mosquitoes* reads like a Penn Station New Year's printout of the last year's lost-and-founds. Yet the most impressive transmogrification (as Faulkner would call it) may be the borrowed triads of professorial abstractions. These, it seems to me, show Faulkner at his most precocious. Astutely, even uniquely, Faulkner picks up two thematic triads from *The Professor's House*. One is the chance-form-utility triad of linked ideas in "Tom Outland's Story," which Professor St. Peter ponders before he almost dies. The second is the art-religion-science triad developed in St. Peter's overheard lecture, which we consider first.

When in *The Professor's House* St. Peter's wife and son-in-law eavesdrop on his class, they hear him teaching that art and religion are the same thing in the end, and have given man the only happiness he ever knew, while science has not added one thing of value to human life beyond comfort. Faulkner appropriates this lecture for *Mosquitoes*, changing *science* to the more general term *education* (St. Peter's field). This change itself, however, echoes another passage in *The Professor's House*, describing Roddy Blake's "great respect for education," though "he believed it was some kind of hocus-pocus that enabled a man to live without work" (PH 188). According to Faulkner's Dawson Fairchild, to some extent modeled on Sherwood Anderson (*New Orleans Sketches*, xxi),

[Education] doesn't make us all brave or healthy or happy or wise, it doesn't even keep us married. In fact, to take on education by the modern process is like marrying in haste and spending the rest of your life making the best of it. But, understand me: I have no quarrel with education. I don't think it hurts you much, except to make you unhappy and unfit for work, for which man was cursed by the gods before they had learned about education. And if it were not education, it would be something else just as bad, and perhaps worse. Man must fill his time some way, you know. (M 41–42)

Cather's Professor St. Peter quarreled with science first and later objected to "the aim to 'show results' that was undermining and vulgarizing education" (PH 140). He said science competed inadequately with art and religion because it offered only ingenious toys, while art or religion provided a sense of human importance, human centrality in life's drama. Faulkner, registering St. Peter's loss of confidence in his educational profession and loss of interest in his marriage, apparently concluded that too much education was the professor's problem. Since St. Peter symbolizes and summarizes the best of Western civilization, Faulkner may well be right. But St. Peter hasn't figured the fact out, even eager as he is to return to his youthful self, who was "a primitive" (PH 265). Cather, on the other hand, seems to be critiquing Western history and civilization,[3] the more effectively because she develops here an *attractive* protagonist while she critiques him, a skill Faulkner masters only later in such figures as Gavin Stevens.

In any event Faulkner's boating party in *Mosquitoes* continues to play with Cather's suggestions about St. Peter's ideas. Indeed, they soon have little else to do, because they play out St. Peter's fantasy: "We should have been picturesquely shipwrecked together when we were young" (PH 94). Even on shore, however, a conversant labeled (like Louie Marsellus) "the Semitic man" (M 37; PH 43) says, "My people produced Jesus, your people Christianized him. And ever since you have been trying to get him out of your church" (M 40). The passage recalls Scott McGregor's laconic comment to the professor: "How you get by the Methodists is still a mystery to me" (PH 70). In passing, Faulkner's analysts label "the Protestant religion" as "the worst of all" (M 42). Upon hearing such apparently negative reflections, novelist Dawson Fairchild asks, "Are you opposed to religion, then—in the general sense, I mean?" His answer: "Certainly not. . . . The only sense in which religion is general is when it benefits the greatest number in the same way. And the universal benefit of religion is that it gets the children out of the house on Sunday morning." To which comes the smart retort, "But education gets them out of the house five days a week" (41).

While St. Peter famously declared, "Art and religion (they are the same thing, in the end, of course)" (PH 69), the echo in *Mosquitoes* is a murmur: "Artistic temperament . . . so spiritual" (20). At one point art and religion appear to be the same thing in the end, however, even on Faulkner's beached yacht: Dawson Fairchild is accused of clinging to "his conviction [about American art] for the old reason: it's good enough to live with and comfortable to die with—like a belief in immortality. Insurance against doubt or alarm" (M 184).

Turning to Cather's second triad of abstractions, Faulkner also tries his hand in *Mosquitoes* at connections to be made between chance, utility, and design. Cather crystallizes these possibilities most succinctly in "Tom Outland's Story," which begins by stressing chance—Tom's job as a call boy who must retrieve men from their games of chance behind the Ruby Light saloon. The theme proceeds through Tom's chance discovery of Cliff City, and ends with his going off to war on the chance that he will find Roddy Blake. Once by chance ensconced on the Blue Mesa, Tom hears Father Duchene describe the cliff dwellers in terms of the useful designs of their lives, *designs* based on *utility*: "Their life, compared to that of our roving Navajos, must have been quite complex. There is unquestionably a distinct feeling for design in what you call the Cliff City. Buildings are not grouped like that by pure accident, though convenience probably had much to do with it. Convenience often dictates very sound design" (PH 219).

The resultant city is recognized by the Catholic priest as "a sacred spot" where people "built themselves into this mesa and humanized it" (221). St. Peter struggles with the same puzzling triad: "All the most important things in his life, St. Peter sometimes reflected, had been determined by chance. His education in France had been an accident. His married life had been happy largely through a circumstance with which neither he nor his wife had anything to do. . . . Tom Outland had been a stroke of chance he couldn't possibly have imagined . . . it was all fantastic" (257).

In the wake of such chances, St. Peter holds on to the useful forms that imply both "cruel biological necessities" (PH 21), which have utility, as well as the valuably comfortable designs of his domestic life. That is, he holds tight to the *utilitarian forms* that by *chance* come to represent patterns or *designs* his life has fallen into. He holds chance, utility, and design together in his mind, to symbolize wholeness, as Melville's Ishmael holds the triad of chance-free will-necessity. It is in such a frame of mind that St. Peter thinks, "His career, his wife, his family, were not his life [a form] at all, but a chain of events [a design] which had happened to him [by chance]. All these things had nothing to do with the person he was in the beginning" (264).

Faulkner shrewdly spots these thematic connections. He sees the clear injunction to deal with them, which is implied in St. Peter's observation that "the human mind, the individual mind, has always been made more interesting by dwelling on the old riddles, even if it makes nothing of them" (PH 68). Faulkner seems determined to make his sculptor Gordon interesting, so Gordon strolls his wharf thinking, "Form and utility. . . . Or form and chance. Or chance and utility" as "he walked, surrounded by ghosts" (M 47). And I, for one, catching sight of all these buzzwords and riddles, acknowledge that Gordon is more interesting to me for dwelling on them. Both writers were right.

In the course of *The Professor's House*, St. Peter concludes that "the design of his life had been the work of this secondary social man, the lover." None of it had anything to do with "his original ego," the "Kansas boy who had come back to St. Peter" (265) during that summer he spends alone. St. Peter concludes that "adolescence grafted a new creature into the original one, and that the complexion of a man's life was largely determined by how well or ill his original self and his nature as modified by sex rubbed on together" (267). Faulkner appears to have taken quite seriously this passage with its implications that sex comes into life as a graft, an intrusion. Gordon, the most sympathetic character among Faulkner's crew, chooses not to get involved personally with intrusive sexual relationships, but to cherish a marble torso and to frequent brothels.

Perhaps the most stunning transfer of material one can imagine between Cather and Faulkner concerns the central metaphor of "Tom Outland's Story." David Harrell observes,

The theme of art saving life from time, paradoxically preserving it in static motion, is the same [in two Cather works]. In *The Song of the Lark*, Cather introduces this theme and explicates it, but not until "Tom Outland's Story" does she develop it fully, creating an entire landscape to contain it. . . . What Outland finds is indeed a sort of natural urn, "a memorial to man's thoughts and works which defy the ravagings of time and attain the immortality of art." . . . Like Keats's speaker, Outland is enthralled by the images before him. . . . It is life once again caught in static motion, "like a fly in amber." (Harrell 140)

That Keatsian urn, therefore that blue mesa landscape's symbolic values, recur repeatedly, as all Faulkner students know, throughout the Yoknapatawpha saga. We see here one reason the image is so highly charged for Faulkner's imagination: he seized it from a master fiction as well as a master poem. As he himself pointed out years later, "If a writer has to rob his mother, he will not hesitate; the *Ode on a Grecian Urn* is worth any number of old ladies" (*Lion* 239).

What Cather's St. Peter finally needs to learn is how to desire again. St. Peter believes, "Desire is creation, is the magical element in that process. If there was an instrument by which to measure desire, one could foretell achievement" (PH 29). If St. Peter could desire it, he could even learn to live without delight, and that is his Everest. He starts haltingly at the end, by desiring Augusta's company in his newfound loneliness, which suggests a newfound need for connection.[4]

We can surmise about William Faulkner that at this beginning of his career, he desired literary achievement and was willing to steal from any old lady to attain his goal. That still leaves open the question, however, as to why, with all his raids on her books to choose from by the end of her life, Cather decided to concentrate especially on *Mosquitoes* in the story she arranged to be her last published word, in the posthumous *The Old Beauty and Others* (1948). The answer will lead us to a glimpse of their mutual audacity, and we'll come back to the fact again later. Here we take our first look, before our final double-take, at Cather's "Before Breakfast." We begin by recalling that by the end of her life, Cather habitually did more than one thing at a time. She practiced layering, allusion, compression, suggestivity, simplification—call it whatever you want. So, as well, did Faulkner.

Cather's last short story describes the walk a man takes before breakfast, on his first morning at his offshore vacation cabin where he is staying alone. When she writes that her protagonist "crossed the first brook on stepping stones . . . for the water was rushing down the deep-cut channel with sound and fury,"[5] she clearly expected at least one reader to come to attention. But William Faulkner, whose personal library at his death included only *The Old Beauty* among Cather's works, may already have been willing to bow in recognition. For the character moving in Cather's story, passing a fallen spruce, has just addressed it aloud: "Hello, Grandfather!" (160). Faulkner likely recognized the greeting as a combination of the "Oleh, Chief, Grandfather" that Sam Fathers uses to pay respects to a giant stag in "The Old People" (GDM 177)[6] and the "Chief, Grandfather" (GDM 314) with which Ike McCaslin salutes a giant snake in "The Bear." That snake, which Faulkner described as "the old one, the ancient and accursed about the earth, fatal and solitary . . . evocative of all knowledge and an old weariness" (GDM 314), was previously spotted around dog town in Cather's *My Ántonia*. Cather's Jim Burden described him first and felt "proud of him, to have a kind of respect for his age and size. He seemed like the ancient, eldest Evil" (MA 47).

Other items Faulkner would recognize also appear on the before-breakfast trail. Faulkner would certainly have heard a direct address in the paragraph immediately to follow that brook and that grandfather: "On another breezy, grassy headland . . . one could stand beside a busy rowan tree" (162). In 1948 the world-famous resident of Rowan Oak must have been sure Cather was addressing him when he proceeded past one more paragraph and read, "This knob of grassy headland with the bushy rowan tree had been his vague objective when he left the cabin" (163). Our immediate task is to deduce why this latest of several shared references to grandfathers is a spruce tree and not a snake or a stag. Faulkner claims a fallen tree for a grandfather only *after* this story, in 1955 in *The Big Woods*, where he added, in an italicized interlude between "The Bear" and "The Old People," a third narrative including the address, "Ole, grandfather." Here a hungry black slave pursued by Indians lies down in a swamp behind a fallen tree to eat the ants crawling up it. Immediately after saluting that tree he is slashed by a cottonmouth that he also addresses as Grandfather. Thus, Faulkner deliberately connects the dots between the ancient fallen tree and the deadly snake. Also, after "Before Breakfast" is printed, Faulkner refers to *Mosquitoes* as "a bad book" (*Lion* 92). Agreeing, Cather twits him here for his mistakes, through her grandfather tree. One previous mistake, she suggests, was allowing two runaways from his grounded boat in *Mosquitoes* to take a wrong turn, land in a swamp, and find there "always those bearded eternal trees like gods regarding without alarm this puny desecration of a silence of air and earth and water ancient when hoary old Time himself was a pink and dreadful miracle in his mother's arms. It was she who found the fallen tree" (174).

Back on Cather's island before breakfast, Grenfell finds a fallen tree, which he has noticed before: "The grandfather was a giant spruce tree that had been struck by lightning (must have been about a hundred years ago, the islanders said)." Grenfell stops to twitch off a twig and is astonished at the tree's resilience, which is entirely accountable: "Well, Grandfather! Lasting pretty well, I should say. Compliments! You get good drainage on this hillside, don't you?" (*OB* 160). Cather's point? Trees are not eternal, nor do they predate time, as Faulkner had suggested in *Mosqui-*

toes. Fallen on a cool Canadian coastline and not in a Louisiana swamp, they can last a century or more if they get good drainage. To endure admirably for a surprisingly long time does not require a tree, or even an island, to predate eternity. All things existing in time are finite, including geology.

In readjusting Faulkner's facts, Cather also straightens out Faulkner's distortion of Professor St. Peter's lecture. She changes the emphasis back from education to science. In "Before Breakfast," Cather's Grenfell also stews about education, as a self-educated man might, and then complains specifically about *science.* Cather seems to reassert her point: it's not general education but science that disturbs one most. Grenfell's "childish bitterness towards 'millions' and professors," she tells us, "was the result of several things. Two of Grenfell's sons were 'professors' . . . [one] a distinguished physicist." Further, "a pleasant and courtly scientist whom he had met on the boat yesterday" (OB 144–45) has ruptured Grenfell's equanimity with scientific facts Grenfell did not wish to know or assimilate—such as the probable age of the island. That overtalkative professor declared that the two ends of the island toward which they were sailing didn't match, but came together by chance to make one mass, from different points of origin. At this juncture Cather plays a professor: she deliberately wrecks Faulkner's imagined equanimity with specific facts that stretch from earth (the island's geology) to the heavens (the planet Venus). But she starts with images of women.

In *Mosquitoes* Faulkner has described a young woman's before breakfast swim: "Up from the darkness of the companionway the niece came, naked and silent as a ghost. She stood for a space, but there was no sound from anywhere, and she crossed the deck and stopped again at the rail, breathing the soft chill mist into her lungs, feeling the mist swaddling her firm simple body with a faint lingering chillness. Her legs and arms were so tan that naked she appeared to wear a bathing suit of a startling white. She climbed the rail. The tender rocked a little under her, causing the black motionless water to come alive, making faint sounds. Then she slid over the stern and swam out into the mist" (*M* 164). In Cather's "Before Breakfast" swim, a young woman approaches the water in a white-lined robe, then drops it to reveal a pink bathing suit. The effect of a naked nymph at water's edge is decidedly similar. Faulkner's niece swims out into mist from a grounded yacht; Cather's daughter swims out from island ground to a rock; but the basic scenes mirror each other.

As Faulkner's Patricia reboards the yacht, "The mist without thinning was filling with light: an imminence of dawn like a glory, a splendor of trumpets unheard" (*M* 166). Cather's revising scene about new light reveals "deep shadow and new-born light, yellow as gold, a little unsteady like other new-born things. It was blinking, too, as if its own reflection of the dewdrops was too bright. Or maybe the light had been asleep down under the sea and was just waking up" (*OB* 160). She erases glory and trumpets and splendor—too purple, it seems, in this blinking moment of golden light.

The early swim completed, Faulkner's Patricia tells an admiring young steward, "Let's get some stuff for breakfast, and beat it. We haven't got all day" (*M* 166). Thereafter they gather a flat box of bacon, a loaf of bread, matches, a knife, and oranges, for Faulkner does not yet trust *suggestion*. When Cather's Grenfell returns to his cabin with sharpened appetite, he smells coffee and that is enough to assure him of his good breakfast ahead.

At this point I would like to compress Faulknerian details myself and concentrate on Venus, the morning star and lofty ideal opposite these earthly daughters who proceed swimmingly. Cather is able to make one image bear many meanings. Her story begins when Henry Grenfell rises in his island cabin after a bad night, raises his bedroom shades and tips his head for eye drops, then spots Venus with his dry eyes. Here the authorial conversation begins, below the earshot of unsuspecting readers, and Cather's first sally accosts Faulkner's facts. For in *Mosquitoes* the narrator has commented, "The moon was getting up, rising out of the dark water: a tarnished, implacable Venus" (133). Her first agenda item is to remind the narrator of *Mosquitoes* that Venus and the moon remain different things: Rising moon goddesses aside, Venus is a planet; planets *have* moons. Soon after the moon, or the morning or evening star (for the planet Venus is labeled both ways), rises in Faulkner's novel, the sun logically follows, the niece and steward gather their breakfast and depart to be lost in the swamp, and Cather parodies Faulkner's youthful hyperbole. Then she moves back to the planet Venus and the fact that *Mosquitoes* begins with three words: "the sex instinct."

Cather uses the planet Venus, I think, to address Faulkner's first-identified theme. Almost as soon as Grenfell spots Venus, he addresses her aloud: "And what's a hundred and thirty-six million years to you, Madam? . . . You were winking and blinking up there maybe a hundred and thirty-six million times before that date they [i.e., geologists who date the island] are so proud of. The rocks can't tell any tales on you. You were doing your stunt up there long before there was anything down here but — God knows what!" (*OB* 144). The first thing to notice is that Cather keeps plenty of physical and psychological space and time between Venus and her protagonist, while she still confronts the *Mosquitoes* opener head-on.

Toward the end of Faulkner's novel, the writer Dawson Fairchild, who delivers many of the arresting lines, remarks about women, "After all they are merely articulated genital organs with a kind of aptitude for spending whatever money you have; so when they get themselves up to look exactly like all the other ones, you can give all your attention to their bodies" (*M* 241). We can divine but not hear on this page Willa Cather's overtone[7] as she thinks, "You want an articulated female genital organ? Try this, then": "She opened her robe, a grey thing lined with white. Her bathing suit was pink. If a clam stood upright and graciously opened its shell, it would look like that. After a moment she drew her shell together—felt the chill of the morning air, probably" (OB 164). Grenfell's first reaction, watching from the cliffs above as he hastily prepares to rescue the damsel, is to be angry: "This is the North Atlantic, girl, you can't treat it like that!" (164). Nevertheless, she does, and even he recalls in the knick of time that it's best not to rescue people that don't need rescuing. Thereafter he walks home feeling his spirits lift: the geologist's daughter "would have a happy day. He knew just how she felt. She surely did look like a little pink clam in her white shell!" (166).

A thrice-repeated assertion in *Mosquitoes* is that "in actual life people will do anything" (181, 228, 255), and anything usually involves the sex instinct. Cather chooses to differ with Faulkner by suggesting that instincts cannot be so antiseptically separated. Sex is an appetite, like hunger. Making the point as he reviews his own life story, Grenfell thinks of himself as a "throw-back to the Year One, when in the stomach was the only constant, never sleeping, never quite satisfied desire" (OB 157).

In *Mosquitoes*, Faulkner holds young women responsible for a great deal of male stress and confusion, as regards the sex instinct, because the women he portrays are so often selfish, infantile, narcissistic, and stupid. At least most of the women in *Mosquitoes* seem most of these things. Cather deliberately creates an alternate type in her geologist's daughter who swims before breakfast. Cather's young woman is a "comely creature who shows breeding, delicate preferences" and is "sweet, but decided" (OB 145–46). That is, she is an animal with sophisticated tastes and clear opinions. "She had lovely eyes, lovely skin, lovely manners" (145). Nobody could accuse Faulkner's mosquito-bitten young women of lovely manners; yet Cather stresses the quality side by side with moral fiber: "There was no one watching her, she didn't have to keep face—except to herself. That she had to do and no fuss about it. She hadn't dodged. . . . She would have a happy day" (166). Cather also may have smirked a bit in graveside advance, to think she hadn't dodged and could rest happy.

Throughout *Mosquitoes*, Faulkner's characters seem torn between attraction and repulsion in regard to each other, especially as sexual creatures. Their strong ambivalence seems to leave them feeling surly. Thus, Cather's story "Before Breakfast" develops a surly character with the Faulknerian name Grenfell — suggesting his Greenfield farm, perhaps, or a fallen grin and a sulky mood (as petulant as a mosquito-plagued guest trapped on that Faulkner yacht *Nausicaa*). At first, Cather's Grenfell truculently spots the planet Venus. The sight "roused his temper so hot that he began to mutter aloud" (*OB* 144). Though the planet suggests balletic grace — "She had come in on her beat, taken her place in the figure" — in Grenfell's mind that very grace contrasts cruelly with his own rabbitlike anxiety: "Merciless perfection, ageless sovereignty. The poor hare and his clover, poor Grenfell and his eye-drops!" (144). Some moments and a summarized lifetime later, Grenfell sees Venus again: "He bethought him of his eye-drops, tilted back his head, and there was that planet, serene, terrible and splendid, looking at him . . . immortal beauty . . . yes, but only when somebody *saw* it, he fiercely answered back!" (158).

So far, Grenfell's planet vitalizes a sophomoric aphorism in Faulkner's *Mosquitoes*, which Cather accepts in order to dramatize: "the thing is merely the symbol of the word" (*M* 130). She makes the thing, the planet Venus, the symbol of the word *sex*, or words with which Faulkner's novel starts: the sex instinct. Then she observes that Venus is ancient; it predates the isolated island Grenfell stands on; it is both immortal beauty and also merciless perfection. It is force, life force, in the Henry Adams sense of Virgin or Venus. It drives males out of the isolation they construct and defend. It shows them sights that lift their depressions, restore their appetites, rekindle delight. It is terrible and splendid, merciless and sovereign. But only if one *sees it*, as Grenfell testily remarks. Without human sight or insight, the words it symbolizes convey youthfully cynical derision, the tone that dominates *Mosquitoes*. As Cather once observed, it makes one feel so grown-up to be bitter.[8]

Though Venus shines above him, Grenfell realizes that "he himself was . . . sitting in his bathrobe by his washstand, limp!" (*OB* 149). Seen with moistened eyes, however, the morning star, the planet Venus, the sex instinct, can remind Grenfell of simple and self-evident delights. In *Mosquitoes*, Talliaferro declaims about "the spirit of youth, of something fine and hard and clean in the world; something we all desire until our mouths are stopped with dust" (*M* 26). Cather's Grenfell, having seen *both* immortal Venus and also an immediate avatar, thinks succinctly, "Plucky youth is more bracing than enduring age" (*OB* 166). Grenfell's train of thought leads him to the life force that draws "that first amphibious frog-toad . . . to hop along" (166). Venus is immortal and sovereign as a symbol of the appetites and reflexes that perpetuate life. Cather seems to say to William Faulkner, this, my friend, is nothing to be "childishly bitter" about. It is joy, and renewal, and wonder, and beauty: the satisfaction of appetite—both of stomach and genitals; a familiar miracle that one sees, on a good day, before breakfast.

At the end of "Before Breakfast," Cather's Grenfell remembers the worst possibility—a cataclysmic disruption requiring a blind assertion of energy, a call on the life force of Venus herself—for survival. He remembers that such catastrophes require struggle without end. And then he remembers that, after all, things could be worse. So Grenfell ends "Before Breakfast" with the declaration William Faulkner said he searched for. Faulkner said in 1966, "I'm trying to say it all in one sentence, between one Cap and one period" (Cowley 14). Grenfell ends the story by saying it all between one cap and one period, and then holds the sentence to four lines: "Anyhow, when that first amphibious frog-toad found his water-hole dried up behind him, and jumped out to hop along till he could find another—well, he started on a long hop."

3

Possession

NOW WE MUST FACE that harder question: why did Willa Cather care so much what Faulkner had done to *The Professor's House* in *Mosquitoes*, since nobody was any longer reading *Mosquitoes* anyway? It was out of print by 1944 when she wrote her story "Before Breakfast." Obviously, these two writers had more unfinished business. What it was and why they had it is the subject of this chapter.

Here are the facts: William Faulkner, under the tutelage of his friend and literary coach Phil Stone, first intended to be a poet. He struggled long and hard to write poetry and eventually collected enough verse to make a volume. After securing a publisher, Phil Stone wrote a short, three-page preface for the collection, mainly to introduce the poet, who was Stone's main interest; the two marketed the volume as *The Marble Faun*. The verse here describes being frozen in a form, like sculpture. The Four Seas Company of Boston brought out the book, which finally arrived on December 15, 1924. Even before the book appeared, however, the two had provided four separate, multipage lists (sent by Stone to Four Seas on October 5, 13, 19, and November 5) of names who should receive publicity flyers and order forms. These names included not only periodicals and newspapers but also individuals as remote as William Howard Taft, and addresses as far afield as

Nova Scotia (Blotner 374). That Willa Cather and several of her friends would have received such a notice is not a stretch. Further, Edith Lewis recounts the fact that Cather was at this time hosting a literary salon on Friday afternoons at 5 Bank Street. Before it grew overcrowded and was abandoned, the salon entertained habitually such founts of current information as woman about town Viola Roseboro' (Lewis 134–35).[1] Roseboro' not only heard all; she told it.

After Faulkner's poetry book finally materialized, Stone acted as agent and sent copies to those who might prove useful. While the fire that later destroyed the Stone house erased many such records,[2] I am guessing that Willa Cather got such a book, or soon possessed a copy, and surveyed it with interested amusement. Then she used it, ostensibly respectfully, but also parodically. The volume she was finishing at the time Faulkner's poetry saw print was *The Professor's House*. Faulkner's poems, of course, should have validated the promise she had acknowledged through his fictionalized lookalike, *Victor Morse*. What his volume of poems actually provoked, I'm suggesting, was the new name *Tom Outland* (for the Outlandish Tom, Tom, the Piper's son). Faulkner's poetic persona, the marble faun, is a Pan, or piper, who outlandishly enough toward the volume's end, plays the violin. Even if Cather was handed this once-rare volume by some well-meaning or amused friend (for it contains enough mixed metaphors to amuse any attentive or sophisticated poetry lover), we can infer that she got hold of it quickly, for immediately she assessed and absorbed it, then assimilated it, her way.

"Tom Outland's Story" is brilliant but also perplexing. Edith Lewis recounts that Willa Cather had called on a Wetherill brother in Mancos as early as 1915, and had heard firsthand the story of Richard Wetherill's discovery of the Cliff City ruins on Mesa Verde (Lewis 94). But the story Cather eventually based on Wetherill family facts was a long time ripening. According to Woodress she *probably* wrote "Tom Outland's Story" at Grand

Manan (where she eventually set "Before Breakfast") in the summer of 1922: "She pulled out of her portfolio a long story she thought had gone to pot and finished it promptly" (Woodress 323). I have no doubt that the story was essentially finished before *The Marble Faun* arrived for additional interpolations. While the revisions that textual parallels suggest may vastly enrich an already brilliant performance, they are added almost entirely at the beginning and ending—that is, after the center had "set."

We know certainly that starting in late spring of 1925, *The Professor's House* was serialized by *Colliers*, to which it had been sold in March.[3] However nearly complete that manuscript had seemed, as the new year of 1925 came in, time was still left in January and February for Cather to seize on Phil Stone's short and florid preface, and to incorporate every word and phrase of it into "Tom Outland's Story." Yet the Stone buzzwords can all be matched in Cather's first fifteen pages, or first two chapters, though they reappear and are reinforced in the last ten pages. Woodress postulates, "Tom Outland is her youthful other self" (375), and I do not disagree.

We know that Cather, as Faulkner, could write with lightning speed, once galvanizing material caught her eye. Certainly she could also ponder material for years and decades until it "ripened"; witness the fact that her last novel, based on childhood memories, took a lifetime as well as a varied set of provocative assault impulses, to start her up. But facts could suddenly electrify her imagination and then make disparate shards cohere into interlocking parts of a coherent design. As Woodress tells the story of *A Lost Lady*,

The idea for the novel had come to her . . . when she was visiting the Hambourgs in Toronto. One day . . . she received a copy of the Red Cloud paper reporting the death of Mrs. Lyra Anderson in Spokane, Washington, on March 21, 1921. Mrs. Anderson had been Mrs. Silas Garber, the wife of the former governor of Nebraska and the leading lady of the town when Cather was growing up. This obituary brought a flood of memories, and after reading the announcement, Cather retired to her room to rest. Up to that moment, she said, she never had thought of writing about Mrs. Garber, but within an hour the story was all worked out in her mind as if she had read it somewhere. This was another epiphany *like those that had produced both O Pioneers! and The Song of the Lark.* (340; my italics)

Edith Lewis gives a similar account of *Death Comes for the Archbishop*: "It may be that many impressions she gathered on her visits to that country had begun to suggest ideas for stories. But no definite design had formed itself in her mind until we went that summer (the summer of 1925) to New Mexico, stopping first in Santa Fé. There, in a single evening, as she often said, the idea of *Death Comes for the Archbishop* came to her, essentially as she afterwards wrote it" (139). We've also seen how quickly Cather could incorporate Faulkner's tall tales, once she saw how they usefully fit her virtually finished novel *One of Ours*. In a flash, authenticating details could become hers. Lewis explains, "She trusted to her memory to retain anything of real interest or importance" (146).

Examples we'll now look at support the fact suggested before, that "Tom Outland's Story" mimics in its first fifteen pages every abstract phrase and concrete word in Phil Stone's preface to *The Marble Faun*. That much, a comparison of the two texts can demonstrate. What I cannot prove is that Stone and Faulkner mailed Cather a copy of the poems. However, as we have already recognized, once he began writing fiction instead of poetry, Faulkner chewed over the 1925 novel containing Outland's tale, as if it were fetched from his own pantry. Even according to Cather herself, "Tom Outland's Story" allowed her "to open the square window and let in the fresh air that blew off the Blue Mesa, and [to highlight] the fine disregard of trivialities which was in Tom Outland's face and in his behaviour" (ow 31–32). What Cather fashioned in "Tom Outland's Story" was not another sketch of the real Bill Faulkner. She prided herself on never repeating herself. It was, however, a graphic—that is, literalized—rendition of the fantasy fellow Phil Stone had described in his preface. Thus, select what classifying label we will, Tom Outland became Cather's second version of William Faulkner.

Stone's preface begins,

These are primarily the poems of youth and a simple heart. They are the poems of a mind that reacts directly to sunlight and trees and skies and blue hills, reacts without evasion or self-consciousness. They are drenched in sunlight and color as is the land in which they were written, the land which gave birth and sustenance to their author. He has roots in this soil as surely and inevitably as has a tree.

They are the poems of youth. One has to be at a certain age to write poems like these. They belong inevitably to that period of uncertainty and illusion. They are as youthful as cool spring grass.

Cather's story emphasizes the *youth* of a "call boy" addressed as "kid" (183). Because he has *a simple heart*, he is interested in a new fellow in his train crew, Roddy Blake (a male caretaker and model in this phallocentric novel who can suggest either Blake's *Songs of Innocence* or his *Songs of Experience*). Roddy has made a bad impression in Pardee, New Mexico (181). Tom *reacts directly* by doing his job: "I started out to hunt up a train crew" (179); but having rounded them up, he returns to see about Blake's winning streak in a poker game. Cather covers her tracks by starting her story at midnight in the card room behind the Ruby Light Saloon. But once Roddy breaks the bank, staggers home drunk, is guarded all night by the watchful call boy, and is forced to eat a hearty Harvey House breakfast the next morning, the two respond to *sunlight* as they "sat in the sun" (184) and agreed to bank the winnings for the future. The *blue hills* of home arrive in two parts, the tantalizing purplish Blue Mesa that dominates the landscape (186) and the blue Mormon Buttes, also in clear sight in the neighborhood (191).[4] Tom describes Roddy *without evasion* as mannerless, dirty, and smelly (180), and himself with *no self-consciousness*: his work over, he drops back to check on the poker game (181) where he trusts all the players but one (183). He is *rooted* in this soil *like a tree*, for he can describe the flat terrain within a fifteen-mile radius: it is a landscape where you can see for miles. When Roddy and Tom are given charge of a herd of cattle and shown their cabin, Tom finds a place to be rooted in, "the sort of place a man would like to stay in forever" (189). Much later, after discovering Cliff City and its remains, a visiting priest speaks of the former occupants as "your tribe" (219, 220), and extends the "rootedness" Tom feels backward in time, for hundreds or thousands of years.

Certainly, Tom's youthful heart knows *uncertainty*. The initial uncertainty about what will happen to Roddy extends through implied uncertainty about himself and what he should do (rather, an easy ability to change or quit jobs or move from place to place, as is convenient). He then becomes uncertain about what happened to the lost tribe of adopted ancestors in Cliff City. But the *illusion* that life is good in his country permeates most of "Tom Outland's Story" so thoroughly that even the air seems deliriously delicious here—one can get drunk on it (200). It is refreshing as the *cool spring grass* on which the cowboys graze their cattle. All of the "Stone words" will stunningly augment and amplify at the end of "Tom Outland's Story." But all are accounted for *by design*, from the beginning pages.

Phil Stone's preface continues with a list of the new poems' defects, which he pointedly associates with youth: "They also have the defects of youth—youth's impatience, unsophistication and immaturity. They have youth's sheer joy at being alive in the sun and youth's sudden, vague, unreasoned sadness over nothing at all" (6). Cather presents Tom's defining *impatience* immediately, when he roughly wakes Roddy up at dawn to demand a hearty breakfast for watchguard payment (183). The *unsophistication* the two share is soon expressed by their arguments over such stale issues as the Dreyfus case, still important to Roddy (187). Tom's *immaturity* is stressed, if obliquely, when he develops pneumonia and is carefully nursed back to health by Roddy, who "ought to have had boys of his own to look after" (186). Tom the narrator adds at this point, by the way, "Nature's full of such substitutions, but they always seem to me sad, even in botany" (186). I now take this curious aside to be an elbow in the side of the *Marble Faun* poet, who seems determined to mention in his poems every tree he has ever read about, whether likely to be found in a pastoral garden of north Mississippi or not. He includes poplars, aspens, beeches, birches, lilac, alder, oak, cedars, pines, dogwood, and pear. Perhaps she makes her grandfather a spruce tree in "Before Breakfast," years later, for the satisfaction of being accurate as well as suggestive or selective about the designated landscape. She eschews botanical substitutions.

In any case, once he has recovered enough health to work outdoors, Tom Outland is exhilarated by the *sheer joy* of living (193–94) and describes their "blue and gold days" (191) when *being alive in the sun* is enough (191). There is the *unreasoned sadness* produced by the tantalizing Blue Mesa itself, of course—"no wonder the thing bothered us and tempted us; it was always before us and was always changing" (193). But the frustration can be shrugged off as *nothing at all*, partially because Tom plans to explore it.

What Cather does about Stone's next paragraph describing the poet's promise is of particular interest. Stone says, "It is seldom that much can be truthfully said for a first book beyond that it shows promise. And I think these poems show promise. They have an unusual feeling for words and the music of words, a love of soft vowels, an instinct for color and rhythm, and—at times—a hint of coming muscularity of wrist and eye" (MF 7). Cather *shows* what these qualities actually sound and look like, when she has her first-person narrator illustrate all of them in one succinct paragraph:

> It was light up there [at the cliff top] long before it was with us [who are in camp; suggesting *promise*]. When I got up at daybreak and went down to the river to get water [observing daily *rhythms*], our camp would be cold and grey, but the mesa top would be red with sunrise [an *instinct for color*], and all the slim cedars along the rocks would be gold—metallic, like tarnished gold-foil [*an unusual feeling for words*]. Some mornings it would loom up above the dark river like a blazing volcanic mountain [a sentence covering *soft vowels*]. It shortened our days, too, considerably. The sun got behind it [*sunlight as muscularity of wrist and eye*] early in the afternoon, and then our camp would lie in its shadow. After a while the sunset colour would begin to stream up from behind it. Then the mesa was like one great ink-black rock against a sky on fire [dramatic, stunning summary]. (192)

Cather seems deliberately to hold back her "southern" links, stressed by Stone in his fifth paragraph, perhaps to tease or tantalize anyone who doubts she can supply such a thing in a Blue Mesa story. Stone says, "The author of these poems is a man steeped in the soil of his native land, a Southerner by every instinct, and more than that, a Mississippian. George Moore said that all universal art became great by first being provincial, and the sunlight and mocking-birds and blue hills of North Mississippi are a part of this young man's very being" (7). Of course, we learn from St. Peter's recollections, and from those tales Tom told Kathleen and Rosamond, that Tom doesn't know exactly how old he is (115), where he is from (though it might be Mississippi), or who his parents were before they as "mover people" died going west (115). But *southern* is a term Cather has personal interest in, and opinions about, being a Virginia native. She redirects the term in "Tom Outland's Story" by stressing *Virginia* as the defining southern state, through the name of a Virginia native, *Virginia Ward*. Miss Ward is a "nice little Virginia girl" (227–28) with "kind eyes and soft Southern voice" (228), as well as "lovely eyes and such gentle ways" (228), whose dialect is suggested by one dropped consonant in "Washin'ton" (229). The blue hills that are a part of Tom's being, of course, are omnipresent in this story. Indeed, as Tom recounts, every night after supper, "climbing the mesa was our staple topic of conversation" (187).

In short, none of the supposedly singular qualities of the poet named William Faulkner, as conjured by Phil Stone, pose a problem for Willa Cather, once she decides to use them in "Tom Outland's Story." His *varied experience* matches Tom's observations made among workingmen (116, 181, 185). His *wide reading* is matched by Tom's Latin and Blake's newspapers. His *quick humor* corresponds to his deft handling of Blake and Blake's social habits. His *flexibility of imagination* produces the instant plan to follow Blake home and make sure he stays safe from harm, plus the determination to follow runaway cattle into the mesa.

One sentence of Stone's would seem to be a stopper: "It is inevitable that traces of apprenticeship should appear in a first book but a man who has real talent will grow, will leave these things behind, will finally bring forth a flower that could have grown in no garden but his own" (7–8). Cather casts a cold eye on the doubt and the obstacle, however, as she remarks in an Emersonian vein that perception is all, and temperament is final. She can make her point by stressing Tom's perception while she characterizes him. So she has Tom Outland reveal the flowers of his singular mind and *garden* when he perceives vegetation he finds significant: "Whether the top was wooded we couldn't see—it was too high above us; but the cliffs and canyon on the river side were fringed with beautiful growth, groves of quaking asps and piñons and a few dark cedars, perched up in the air *like the hanging gardens of Babylon*" (TOS 192; my italics). Emerging from the mind and mouth of Tom Outland, the simile doesn't even draw attention to itself.

There is left to acknowledge only the oddly familiar relationship between an experienced older man and a younger "apprentice." Roddy and Tom curiously mirror Stone and Faulkner, from the initial guardianship of the younger male's health to the "bankrolling" of his enterprises, especially through the elder's uncanny prowess at poker, to the eventual hurtfulness of the elder's being treated as a hired hand, and to his later exclusion from the spot where a whole civilization is unearthed and reconstructed. I don't try to explain such prophetic accuracy, I merely acknowledge it.

From the start, *youth* is Stone's repetitious key word to describe his fantasy figure. Cather stresses the quality of youth by saying of her "autobiographical" Professor St. Peter, "His misfortune was that he loved youth . . . he was weak to it, it kindled him" (PH 88). Within "Tom Outland's Story" Cather allows Tom to explain of his friend Roddy Blake, "What . . . [Roddy] needed was a pal, a straight fellow to give an account to. I was ten years younger and that was an advantage" (PH 185). Certainly in this case, life seems to imitate art. Yet once again, whether in *Collier's* or in book form, William Faulkner recognized his own material, even his own silhouette, in Willa Cather's work. On the one hand, this was a profoundly flattering and idealized sketch that followed Stone's sentimentalizing lead. On the other hand, seeing the material included in so brilliant a novel had to be maddening. Even a much more secure man might have felt used. The woodcut-like outline may have gone to Faulkner's head momentarily, however, for what Faulkner seems to have tried elaborating in *Mosquitoes* is the undercurrent of negation and disgust that is also a shadowside of Professor St. Peter. From the second page, when the professor recalls almost a lifetime of leaping into his tin bathtub "to give it another coat of the many paints that were advertised to behave like porcelain, and didn't" (*PH* 12), the American life in which the professor is complicit is just a bit sleazy. It includes shoddy bathtubs, creaky stairs, a badly ventilated attic, ostentatious emeralds, and second-rate colleagues such as Lily Langtry and Professor Crane. It's the sleaze factor, unremittingly underscored in *Mosquitoes*, that sinks Faulkner's *Nausicaa*. But his temptation must have been great, and Faulkner no more resisted it than Outland resisted the impulse to punish Roddy Blake and gain exclusive possession of his Blue Mesa for a whole glorious summer. Already the question is, who has exclusive possession of a sacred spot? Both writers will return to this question.

In any case, what Stone's preface provided Willa Cather was the sketch of a personality who is exactly opposite Professor St. Peter. He is the "primitive" that St. Peter once recalls being, who "was earth, and would return to earth. When white clouds blew over . . . he felt satisfaction and said to himself merely: 'That is right.' Coming upon a curly root that thrust itself across his path, he said: 'That is it'" (265–66). And while St. Peter continues to charm my irony-loving academic heart, he failed to delight his creator, even after she had made him startlingly similar to herself. She called this volume "a nasty, grim little tale" (Woodress 367) and labeled the book in a gift volume inscribed to Robert Frost as "a story of letting go with the heart" (CCC Drew). Even before *My Mortal Enemy* was published in 1926, Cather was fashioning a faux interview to move her readers along towards the more positive *Death Comes for the Archbishop* (CCC Drew; Porter). The evidence suggests that she pounced on Stone's preface in order to enhance her alternative character who would serve as relief to Professor St. Peter. "Just when the morning brightness of the world was wearing off for him, along came Outland and brought him a kind of second youth" (*PH* 258).

Cather then captures in Tom the direct, forthright, youthful, and simple heart that Phil Stone claimed to know—even, however improbably, to call William Faulkner. That figure emerges in both the style and the contents of the abrupt opening to her own "Tom Outland's Story": "The thing that side-tracked me and made me so late coming to college was a somewhat unusual accident, or string of accidents. It began with a poker game when I was a call boy in Pardee, New Mexico." At the beginning of this story, Cather relies consistently on subject-verb-object sentences of the kind that simple, unevasive hearts would use. She avoids adjectives and shaded or nuanced declarations until the end of the story, when Tom has lost his innocence through the mutual betrayals of which he accuses himself and Roddy. Cather also, for future reference, "realistically" depicts a high-stakes poker game. It doesn't seem an accident that William Faulkner later fashions a poker game in "Was" that is so complicated, even professionals have a hard time following what is happening (I've asked a couple for help and they couldn't). Susan Snell, in fact, identifies the significant determining hand with one Phil Stone told of playing (85). When Faulkner shows Cather how to play—or even write about—poker, cards are stuffed up sleeves *by design, because* it is a real game of chance on which ride matters of importance: who will end up playing what game. That "Was" is the unexpectedly comic beginning of *Go Down, Moses*, a "serious" book by its end, is a matter of importance to us and to this book.

Cather's Tom Outland, however, remains an honest type, up until he admits lying to win an argument with Roddy (TOS 243). And Stone's preface associates *his* subject, the poet William Faulkner, with "unflinching honesty" (MF 8). Then the preface ends on the word *honest*; it's a bizarre insistence on Stone's part, perhaps not unlike bluffing at poker. The protesting-too-much may have provided an eyebrow-raiser for an amused Willa Cather. But "What's honest?" remains an important and open question hereafter, and both writers address it, more than once.

In "Tom Outland's Story," once Tom guards Roddy's *gold*

through the night, in his room behind a *sky-blue* door in the yellow quarter, and dawn arrives, Cather is free to use color her own way: "The sun came up and turned the 'dobe town *red* in a minute" (PH 182; my italics). Her way, we note here, first dwells on *primary* colors that convey a primary event or development, as a simple heart might register it. Even when Cather begins to break loose, depicting Tom's exhilarated delight in life on the range, the shadow of the Blue Mesa provides an equivalent for Stone's blue hills of Mississippi. And Tom's prose remains simple, direct, in look-see-say format: "The Blue Mesa was one of the landmarks we always saw from Pardee—landmarks mean so much in a flat country. To the northwest, over toward Utah, we had the Mormon Buttes, three sharp blue peaks that always sat there. The Blue Mesa was south of us, and was much stronger in colour, almost purple. People said the rock itself had a deep purplish cast. It looked from our town, like a naked blue rock set down alone in the plain, almost square, except that the top was higher at the end" (186). We'll soon watch Faulkner reappropriate this southwestern landscape for Mississippi, by making Dilsey's yard, in *The Sound and the Fury*, remind one of Mexican adobe walls shaped by hand.

Father Duchene intensifies Tom's sense of belonging, of being rooted here as Phil Stone said his poet was rooted, with the comment, "I am inclined to think that your tribe were a superior people" (PH 219). Duchene adds, "There is evidence on every hand that they lived for something more than food and shelter. . . . There is unquestionably a distinct feeling for design, . . . though convenience probably had much to do with it" (PH 219). The priest elaborates, "I see your tribe as a provident, thoughtful people, who made their livelihood secure by raising crops and fowl. . . . I see them here, isolated, off from other tribes, working out their destiny. . . . Your people were cut off here without the influence of example or emulation, with no incentive but some natural yearning for order and security. They built themselves into this mesa and humanized it" (*PH* 220–21). The insistent *your people* phrase also amplifies Stone's remarks.

Those who find in this priestly (i.e., truthful) account of 1925 a startling blueprint for a Yoknapatawpha saga—complete with all the positive suggestions inherent in words such as *design, provident, thoughtful, raising crops and fowl, isolated, working out their destiny, yearning for order and security, humanized*—must take heed of *all* the details included. Given enough anger in the inspecting imagination, Cliff City also provocatively furnishes "corncobs everywhere, and ears of corn with the kernels still on them" (*PH* 249–50). Thus, the mesa can also suggest the impotent assaults of a Popeye in *Sanctuary*—suddenly a very striking novel title indeed for a story that includes brutal rape of "a sacred spot." One sees that a word repeated to characterize Faulkner's marble faun is *impotent* or *impotence* (19, 36, 45). Perhaps Cliff City suggested a way for Faulkner to challenge Cather to top that.

After Tom Outland has made some effort through newspaper advertisements to contact his exiled friend, Roddy Blake, whom he has effectively expelled from their storied paradise (as Faulkner later expelled Phil Stone [Snell 203–4]), he returns to the mesa alone as "sole owner and proprietor." He's openly, not secretively, glad about it. But his observing eye is now in a shadow. He describes with newly sophisticated syntax and nuance the hellishly red light bathing the scene he glories in. We notice embedded in the scene that figure of sun and moon facing each other across the earth. Cather has formerly used the display in both *My Ántonia* and *One of Ours* to suggest opposition or opposite things and complex contrasts:

I'll never forget the night I got back. I crossed the river an hour before sunset and hobbled my horse in the wide bottom of Cow Canyon. The moon was up, though the sun hadn't set, and it had that glittering silveriness the early stars have in high altitudes. The heavenly bodies look so much more remote from the bottom of a deep canyon than they do from the level. The climb of the walls helps out the eye, somehow. I lay down on a solitary rock that was like an island in the bottom of the valley, and looked up. The grey sage-brush and the blue-grey rock around me were already in shadow, but high above me, the canyon walls were dyed flame-colour with the sunset, and the Cliff City lay in a gold haze against the dark cavern. [Note that the primary blue-red-gold now shades into greys and hazy, nuanced shadows.] In a few minutes, it, too, was grey, and only the rim rock at the top held the red light. When that was gone, I could still see the copper glow in the pinions along the top ledges. The arc of the sky over the canyon was silvery blue, with its pale yellow moon, and presently stars shivered into it, like crystals dropped into perfectly clear water. (250)

Tracing this subtle use of color alone, through "Tom Outland's Story," suggests that by this point in her career, Cather could more or less do anything. She finds a way to include it all. St. Peter, for example, has said that in Tom's world there were no shadows. Yet when Tom is in Washington and taking the secretary of the director of the Smithsonian to lunch, he doesn't need shadows to report, "I was amazed and ashamed that a man of fifty, a man of the world, a scholar with ever so many degrees, should find it worth his while to show off before a boy, a boy of such humble pretensions, who didn't know how to eat the *hors d'oeuvres*" (231). Shadows, we see, are ephemeral; negative judgments don't require them.

Phil Stone closes his brief preface with the much-quoted anecdote: "On one of our long walks through the hills, I remarked that I thought the main trouble with Amy Lowell and her gang of drum-beaters was their *eternal* damned self-consciousness, that they always had one eye on the ball and the other eye on the grandstand. To which the author of these poems replied that his personal trouble as a poet seemed to be that he had one eye on the ball and the other on Babe Ruth." We begin to understand the consequences of his glances. What we haven't understood is that Cather, who played hardball the same way he did, could also keep an eye on the grandstand, where she could imagine the presence of the Babe Ruth of the future. Having picked the lad out and "anointed" him, however, she felt more than passing interest and responsibility for what he would make of his talent. She thought *Mosquitoes* a very poor use of it, and said so in "Before Breakfast." Faulkner agreed, as both agreed that the effort of *The Sound and the Fury* was different, was living water, a stream of life, something worth traversing carefully, with stepping stones. But then, as the story "Before Breakfast" concedes, when even a churl sees plucky youth do something just right, without balking, it's worth getting up early for. Saluting the feat, she, he, we can have a happy day.

4

The Sounds Become Fury

IN 1928, THE YEAR FOLLOWING the publication of *Death Comes for the Archbishop*, Faulkner was working on his great novel *The Sound and the Fury*, and he snatched for it whatever he pleased. At the least, he reived from Cather's *My Ántonia*, *A Lost Lady*, *My Mortal Enemy*, and *Death Comes for the Archbishop*. In fact, he folded a remarkable number of their details into the coalescing new work. The surprise is that, so far as I can see, he used nothing from *One of Ours* and *The Professor's House*. He may have felt he had exhausted those two already.

The important thing to note, however, is the *quality* of Faulkner's appropriations and inversions and nose-thumbing pirouettes. That quality has increased exponentially—almost miraculously. If nothing else, his "thefts" (his word) are his way of showing he can triumph when his work is compared to that Catherian tour de force and "novel démeublé" *My Mortal Enemy*, published in 1926. He may have decided, in fact, that he—like Myra Henshawe—had spotted a mortal enemy who could be both beloved and an enemy, too. The juxtaposed recognition of threat and a concomitant sense of miracle derives from his rapidly ascending style, more than content. For example, Benjy's love of a mirror mirrors the opening of *My Mortal Enemy*, in which the narrator sees her subject Myra in a mirror that reflects another mirror. To a spectator in the grandstand, the comparisons can become dizzying, as in a hall of mirrors. At the least, narrator Nellie Birdseye spots in her Catherian mirror what she finds most magnetic, most awesome, and most frightening; she sees in the mirror what grips her attention most—that middle-aged figure who not only controls this story but also tells all the best hometown stories. The ominous possible fact—that what frightens one most may mirror the self—will return to both writers.

In *The Sound and the Fury*, Faulkner retrieves his French title—"Une Ballade des Femmes Perdues"—from Cather's *A Lost Lady*. He thereafter said his novel was about "two lost ladies," doubling the value of the snatch-back, as became his practice. More substantially, he then picked up *all* the salient features of *My Ántonia* and quite brilliantly incorporated them as his own. Juxtaposing the two masterpieces, *My Ántonia* and *The Sound and the Fury*, allows any responsive reader to compare the unique strengths of both geniuses, as well as the advantages to be gained from attentiveness to literary influence.

The ever-more-widely acclaimed *My Ántonia*,[1] which we know Phil Stone ordered in 1922,[2] gave Faulkner the names Burden and Bundren.[3] Besides the name *Burden*, the name *Lena* also turns up later in *Light in August*.[4] But first, Cather's *My Ántonia* taught Faulkner the splendid effects to be achieved by using both linear and cyclical structural organizations simultaneously.[5] That is, *My Ántonia* proceeds chronologically, in linear sequence, while each interior book is cyclical and covers a whole year's round. Similarly, disordered sections of *The Sound and the Fury* can be reshuffled into the linear sequence of a Thursday-through-Sunday Easter weekend, while each narrator's section covers one day's cycle. In short, Faulkner takes from *My Ántonia* the advantages to be gained when one uses natural cycles—whether daily, seasonal, or yearly—to shape each component of the novel: each book of Cather's novel not only covers a year but also starts in a different season; each book of Faulkner's novel mixes years as memory will do, while actually covering only one day in an Easter week. In *The Sound and the Fury* as well as in *As I Lay Dying* and *Absalom, Absalom!* Faulkner mixes linear and cyclical structures effectively, having seen how to do it in *My Ántonia*.

Moreover, in *The Sound and the Fury*, one *Ántonia*-based structuring device is tripled: Faulkner has *three* men tell the story of one woman, a sisterlike figure who centrally shaped their lives. Further, *My Ántonia* starts twice (as *Death Comes for the Archbishop* does also); and Faulkner's tour de force then *doubles* the fun by starting over four times, in each new section. Faulkner thus keeps multiplying the tricks a structure can provide, keeps structuring in multiples, and seems to double the speed of the performance. He also, to say it another way, amplifies the ironies achievable when a sensitive young man, cut loose from his roots, appropriates another's story, or a female story, for his own — for his *my* thing. That happens in both *My Ántonia* and *The Sound and the Fury*. Faulkner will repeat the device again when Quentin follows Miss Rosa Coldfield's lead and then appropriates — only to transgender it — a female's story in *Absalom, Absalom!* That is, he starts with a female's story and makes it compellingly macho male, perhaps male squared, counting Sutpen's sons. Quentin also illustrates, as does Jim Burden, what observable results can occur when a sensitive young man tries to possess a strong, older-seeming, and unavailable but beloved young woman, for his exclusive possession. That effort would make her his owned object, of course, and therefore would make his rejection or rebuff, assuming she's a strong young woman, more likely.

Then there are the kaleidoscopic possibilities to be exploited when a particular family functions as a symbolic "family of man." Such a unit — Faulkner's Compsons and Cather's Shimerdas — includes a self-destructive father, a self-absorbed and self-pitying mother, a fallen daughter, a vulnerable younger female child, an idiot, a male suicide, and a greedy son the mother values most. In both novels those "families of man" are made up of four children, a configuration *both* writers will soon change by expanding. Cather will expand the family to a whole Catholic church (the children of God) in *Death Comes for the Archbishop,* and Faulkner will expand it to the Bundrens (another family of man) in *As I Lay Dying.* With my apologies to classical reference, the title of *As I Lay Dying* seems to me to reference Cather's last book: *Death Comes for the Archbishop.* After *As I Lay Dying* is published, Cather will adopt its family of man for "Old Mrs. Harris": one daughter and four sons. For the present, these families stand in contrast to another family: *orphan* Jim lives comfortably with his grandparents instead of in a crowded dugout in the earth, in *My Ántonia,* while the white Compsons contrast to the black Gibsons, of equal number, in *The Sound and the Fury.* But Faulkner multiplies techniques; so while the Gibsons numerically match the Compsons, Quentin also matches Orphan Jim when he thinks wistfully, "If I'd had a mother so I could say Mother, Mother" (*SF* 172). Both young men feel isolated and alone.

Both novels feature grasping brothers like Ambrosch and Jason who will cheat to amass more money, who are recognized as "too mean" (*MA* 78), and who will hurt themselves in order to punish others or to acquire more wealth; further, these vicious brothers are their socially inferior mothers' delights and comforts, a fact denoting their inferior or lower characters. In both novels the beloved woman is linked to trees, perhaps trees of life: Caddy smells like trees to Benjy, while Ántonia's hand on an orchard tree suggests her goodness and fertility. And the idiot brothers in both novels are eventually sent to mental institutions, because both "naturals" are thought to threaten violence, though both are first said to be harmless and lovable.

The central or primary female figure in each novel does not tell her own story but is rather presented through the eyes of a brotherly lover (or two). Yet both these beloved women are children's leaders and game-organizers, associated with strength and strong will. Conversely, committing suicide in each novel is associated with a man's dressing cleanly and neatly first, and then saving from damage what clothes and precious possessions he can. Again, both novels feature centrally the servants who love children better than anyone else can. Both include little girls—Yulka Shimerda or Nina Harling in Cather's novel; and Julio's sister or young Caddy in Faulkner's—who play essentially comic roles that are often nonspeaking, nonchalantly self-serving, and enigmatic. One notes in passing that the man Cather boasted of finding most attractive to her was named Julio (Stout, *Writer* 124–25). Both Julios startle by bounding surprisingly into our consciousness from some spot in a peripheral vision.

Both novels develop thematically the results when an older way of life disintegrates. Friendly Bohemia cannot be replicated for Mr. Shimerda in Nebraska, and the likes of patriarchal General Compson will not be seen again in Mississippi. Further, both novels exploit the helplessness of trusting people before the rapacious mendacity of Wick Cutter or Jason Compson. These two characters are evil to the core, as both writers proudly pointed out. Yet both novels end in some sense on an upbeat note, to bring off which Faulkner starts Dilsey's section with a reference to or a paraphrase of the Twenty-third Psalm.

The Lord is my shepherd: I shall not want.

He maketh me to lie down in green pastures; he leadeth me beside the still waters.

He restoreth my soul: he leadeth me in the paths of righteousness for his name's sake.

Yea, though I walk through the valley of the shadow of death, I will fear no evil: for thou art with me; thy rod and thy staff they comfort me.

Thou preparest a table before me in the presence of mine enemies; thou anointeth my head with oil; my cup runneth over.

Surely goodness and mercy shall follow me all the days of my life; and I will dwell in the house of the Lord forever.

The tip-off to this biblical parallel comes in the crucial last words or phrase of this fourth section's first sentence: "The day dawned bleak and chill, a moving wall of grey light out of the northeast which, instead of dissolving into moisture, seemed to disintegrate into minute and venomous particles, like dust that, when Dilsey opened the door of her cabin and emerged needled laterally into her flesh, precipitating not so much a moisture as a substance partaking of the quality of thin, not quite congealed oil." The rest of the psalm falls into place—Dilsey's faith, the Compson's pasture, the food she cooks in the Compson kitchen, her stead-fast resilience, her ability to prepare each Compson for burial in turn, her living in the presence of her enemy Jason—once one has the oil-like particles that initially dampen her head and flesh. Faulkner learned from Cather (who learned from Henry James who learned from Poe) to plant his most important word in the final position of the first sentence. Once the emphasized oil on the head is accounted for, the shepherding, green pastures, paths of righteousness, shadow of death, prepared table, good-ness, and mercy, all "take their place in the figure," as in "Before Breakfast."

Crucially, both novels end with finale passages that are major tours de force, each encompassing everything—that is, both jag-gedness and smooth order; both immediate time and all time. In fact, all the opposites that each writer has developed throughout each novel are implied or explicitly present. And both final pas-sages are justly famous, while they grippingly suggest many of the same concepts.

For Ántonia and me, this had been the road of Destiny; had taken us to those early accidents of fortune which predeter-mined for us all that we can ever be. Now I understood that the same road was to bring us together again. Whatever we had missed, we possessed together the precious, the incom-municable past.

Luster looked quickly back over his shoulder, then he drove on. The broken flower drooped over Ben's fist and his eyes were empty and blue and serene again as cornice and façade flowed smoothly once more from left to right, post and tree, window and doorway and signboard each in its ordered place.

Movement, order, a return to the past that dictates the future, predetermined destiny and the roads that lead to it, the incommunicable past, all appear in both splendid finishes, which balance symmetrically.

When one looks at the parallels between *My Ántonia* and *The Sound and the Fury*, the mass of evidence makes a clear case for deliberate—and successful—one-upmanship. The comparisons imply conscious competition. Yet it was *Death Comes for the Archbishop* that provided the adrenalin rush for this imperative effort to start with. The very improbability of Faulkner's swift assimilation of its peaks and valleys shows how seriously annoyed he was becoming—and how engaged he now was in seizing the crown for his own. As Mr. Compson comments in laconic semaphore signal, "It used to be a gentleman was known by his books; nowadays he is known by the ones he has not returned" (81). When Faulkner stole them, he kept them.

Since *Death Comes for the Archbishop* was published in the year before Faulkner wrote *The Sound and the Fury* in 1928, one would probably assume that he had not read the Cather work before writing his best-known masterpiece, were it not for their now-clarifying history and for the number of cuttings he took from Cather's newest narrative, to graft into his novel in progress. Critics protested the unconventionality of both books. The first tip-off that *Death Comes for the Archbishop* was to be one of his salient sources is his description of Dilsey's cabin: "The earth immediately about the door was bare. It had a patina, as though from the soles of bare feet in generations, like old silver or the walls of Mexican houses which have been plastered by hand"

(266). The cabin setting is also reminiscent of the furnishings for Archbishop Latour's beloved study in his adobe house in Santa Fe. His room is lighted by "silver candlesticks ["old silver"] he had brought from France long ago" (35), and enclosed by "thick clay walls . . . finished on the inside by the deft palms of Indian women," and blessed by "that irregular and intimate quality of things made entirely by the human hand" ["walls of Mexican houses which have been plastered by hand"] (DCA 33–34). Its furniture had been "bought from the departed Mexican priest" [perhaps, like Father Jesus de Baca, someone who teaches us to value *parrots* (86)] (DCA 34).

The early section of *Death Comes for the Archbishop*, entitled "The Vicar Apostolic," seems particularly to have fertilized Faulkner's imagination, much as Stone's preface is recycled in the first pages of Cather's "Tom Outland's Story." Another image soon arrests Faulkner's attention after Latour emerges from his study to feast with Father Vaillant on Christmas Day. (Dilsey, of course, starting from her similar private space or site, celebrates Easter in a church decorated with a signal Christmas bell.) Cather's two priests begin to remember their hometown and find that "their thoughts met in that tilted cobble street winding down a hill, . . . a lonely street after nightfall, with soft street lamps shaped like lanterns at the darkest turnings" (DCA 42). That French street soon reappears as Quentin's recurrent memory of his Mississippi home: "The street lamps . . . go down the hill then they rise toward town like lanterns hung one above another on a wall" (SF 100).

Another interesting item appeals to Faulkner, as Cather's Latour remembers being "carried out of the body thus to a place far away. It had happened in a street in New Orleans.[6] He had turned a corner and come upon an old woman with a basket of yellow flowers; sprays of yellow sending out a honey-sweet perfume. . . . He was overcome by a feeling of place, and was dropped, cassock and all, into a garden in the south of France where he had been sent one winter in his childhood to recover from an illness" (*DCA* 43). Faulkner's Quentin, of course, is repeatedly carried out of the body to a place far away where he spent his childhood, occasionally recovering from such misfortunes as a broken leg and smelling the "honey-sweet perfume" of honeysuckle. In fact, when he remembers his youth, he's always "getting honeysuckle all mixed up in it" (*SF* 129). Both instantly overwhelming memories of childhood mix sweet smells with pain to become "a voice weeping steadily and softly beyond the twilit door the twilight-colored smell of honeysuckle" (*SF* 95).

Other interesting images from Cather's 1927 masterpiece pop up in Faulkner's first clear-cut masterpiece of 1929. For example, the pregnant Caddy (a word for one who carries clubs) marries in April, when apple blossoms appear in Mississippi; and Quentin wakes in Massachusetts to remember Caddy's wedding and murmur distractedly, "The month of brides" (*SF* 77). When he remembers Caddy's "running already . . . out of the mirror like a cloud, her veil swirling" (81) at the wedding, Quentin suddenly thinks, "The odor of apple tree her head against the twilight her arms behind her head kimono-winged the voice that breathed o'er eden clothes upon the bed by the nose seen above the apple" (105–6). Quentin's linking of special month, sweet-smelling apple blossoms, mirror reflections, voices breathing o'er eden, and brides, makes a vividly new sense when his cluster of associations is juxtaposed with this passage from *Death Comes for the Archbishop*:

It was the month of Mary and the month of May. . . . The apple trees were in blossom, the cherry blooms had gone by. The air and the earth interpenetrated in the warm gusts of spring. . . . The air one breathed was saturated with earthy smells, and the grass under foot had a reflection of blue sky in it.

. . . This was a very happy season for Father Vaillant. For years he had not been able properly to observe this

month which in his boyhood he had selected to be the holy
month . . . dedicated to the contemplation of his Gracious
Patroness.

. . . All the most important events in his own history had occurred in the blessed month when this sinful and sullied world
puts on white . . . and becomes, for a little, lovely enough to be
in truth the Bride of Christ. (200–204)

In short, Faulkner is doing to Cather's novel exactly what Cather
did to Phil Stone's preface.

It was not merely images and fragments, however, but also
themes (inspirations) that Faulkner argued young writers should
pick up from what they read. Repeatedly, I have gasped with admiration when I realized the implications of what Faulkner apparently *saw* in Cather, for he seems to me to have been as subtly perceptive and insightful a reader as she ever acquired. When
considering what *The Sound and the Fury* has to teach about its
assimilated immediate predecessor, *Death Comes for the Archbishop*, I find myself redefining Cather's novel more frequently
than I re-vision Faulkner's.

For example, most readers have no difficulty defining *The
Sound and the Fury* as a novel about loss, especially after Faulkner
described it repeatedly as "the tragedy of two lost women: Caddy
and her daughter" (*Lion* 222). We have understood it in terms
of loss of a beloved sister, loss of life, loss of hope, loss of patri-
mony, loss of status, loss of a code of behavior, loss of an effective
parent, and so on — for each Compson loses what that Compson
values most. When Faulkner's novel is juxtaposed with *Death
Comes for the Archbishop*, however, Cather's lyrical novel also
seems a treatment of loss. Its title calls attention to irrevocable
loss through death, and its final sentence ends as "the old Archbishop lay before the high altar in the church he had built." The
prologue begins with only an hour of sunlight left, reminding
us that Faulkner, dating the first page of his manuscript April 7,

1928, headed it with the working title *Twilight* (Blotner 569).[7] Almost immediately, Cather's novel develops the story of the lost El Greco. That puzzling anecdote becomes essential if it is taken to state a theme: even valuable and beautiful things can be lost forever; thus, the question we ask of life is how to live with loss. In the course of the narrative, Latour loses his hopeful faith, just before Christmas, and toward the end Father Vaillant must defend his good faith in Rome, for he loses the trust of the Vatican. In fact, the novel proper *starts* with young Father Latour hopelessly lost in a nightmare landscape.

Once this theme becomes visible, I, who missed it for years, wonder how much more emphatically Cather could signal a primary concern than in title, first sentence, last sentence, first narrative, and first action. I think this emphasis conveys Cather's conviction that before the ecstatic joys of the two bishops' lives—both lost for His sake—can be appreciated, one must acknowledge irreparable loss. As Wallace Stevens, another Cather reader, put it when he got it right, "Death is the mother of beauty." The theme also suggests, however, how shrewdly the matured Faulkner read Cather, and how naturally he could summarize a novel about two lost women, once he had started by assimilating a novel about loss featuring two men who experience it constantly.

The first difference in the treatment of loss in these two novels, of course, is that Cather's contrasting protagonists not only lose but also find. Both Latour and Vaillant dramatize the Bible verse "He that loseth his life for my sake will find it" (Matt. 10:39), as well as William James's dictum: "By their fruits ye shall know them, not their roots" (Skaggs, "Cather's Varieties" 104). Faulkner's fruitless Compsons seem only to lose; yet Dilsey, whose family, or at least whose grandson Luster, "got jes es much Compson devilment in you es any of em" (*SF* 276), finds as useful a life, by losing it in service to others, as Cather's bishops do. The bishops and Dilsey find their lives the same way—by losing them.

In the archbishop's thirsty desert as the action begins, an interesting difference in losses will emerge: Cather's Latour absentmindedly loses himself in space, while Faulkner's Quentin intentionally loses himself in time. Latour "had lost his way, and was trying to get back to the trail, with only his compass and his sense of direction for guides. The difficulty was that the country in which he found himself was so featureless—or rather, that it was crowded with features, all exactly alike" (17). Quentin, conversely, remarks wryly, "But then I suppose it takes at least one hour to lose time in, who has been longer than history getting into the mechanical progression of it" (SF 83). Yet time refuses to be lost, and so "time is your misfortune Father said" (SF 104). Thus, the biblical admonishments concerning losing and finding continue and ironies abound.

The theme of loss is also connected to another theme Faulkner found in the opening pages of *Death Comes for the Archbishop*. Cather's prologue begins with three cardinals and a bishop enjoying a famously fine view in which "below the balustrade was the drop into the air, and far below the landscape stretched soft and undulating; there was nothing to arrest the eye until it reached Rome itself" (3). That is, they look off into the air until their eyes reach the Eternal City. Similarly, Quentin and his father consider "the long diminishing parade of time you didn't hear. Like Father said down the long and lonely light-rays you might see Jesus walking, like. And the good Saint Francis that said Little Sister Death, that never had a sister" (SF 76). Cather's lost El Greco, we register, was a portrait depicting "a St. Francis, of almost feminine beauty" (like a little sister) (DCA 12).

Another thematic overlap concerns self-absorption or self-consciousness. Cather's Latour, when lost in the terrible desert, "blotted himself out of his own consciousness and meditated upon the anguish of his Lord" (DCA 20), after which he was saved. Reversing the pattern just before he dies, "he sat in the middle of his own consciousness; none of his former states of mind were lost or outgrown. They were all within reach of his hand, and all comprehensible" (DCA 290). Latour's state of mind just preceding his death could as easily describe Quentin Compson's. In their last days, both sit in the centers of their consciousness where all former states of mind are within reach of a hand. Then both die.

Still another dominant theme in both these novels is the need for and longing for order. Most critics recognize by now that all sections of *The Sound and the Fury* are ordered not only by a morning-to-evening time progression but also by such recurrent images as bells, smells, and food. These patterns find interesting precedents in *Death Comes for the Archbishop*. The new bishop, the cardinals are told, "must be a man to whom order is necessary—as dear as life" (DCA 8), especially since the church in the Southwest is in a state of total disorder, with the old mission churches "in ruins" (DCA 7). In Cather's prologue, the cardinals of Europe enjoy among aromatic "potted orange and oleander trees" (3) their good food and wine, their splendid view which includes the "[bell] dome of St. Peter's" (4), while they hear of the "peculiar horror" of the Southwest desert, where "the very floor of the world is cracked open" (7). Thus, several ordering images —and disordered realities—of *both* novels are set firmly in the first six pages of Cather's book. Cather's churchmen, as do all of Faulkner's characters, "watch the evening coming on" (DCA 13), as if "That Evening Sun" goes down. Cather's novel then starts over again in chapter 1; and Faulkner, catching the step, doubles the effect by beginning four times instead of twice, for the evening sun has sunk repeatedly.

The opening sequences of *Death Comes for the Archbishop* appear to have had a vitalizing power for Faulkner's imagination. When the novel proper begins, Bishop Latour finds himself lost in a hellish, burning desert, a "geometrical nightmare" from which he cannot escape "the intrusive omnipresence of the triangle" (18).[8] Latour's literal burning hell mirrors Benjy's hellish world, and the hellish world prurient Jason creates for himself and others while his head burns. But Latour's literal predicament also equals Quentin's metaphorical dilemma: Quentin would gladly achieve a permanent order while burning in Hell with Caddy for eternity, could he only escape in those isolating flames the "intrusive omnipresence of the triangles" Dalton Ames or other of Caddy's lovers would make after joining them (*SF* 79).

After he is saved, Latour is entertained in a Mexican villa, where he sees a flock of goats that "brought to mind the chapter in the Apocalypse, about the whiteness of them that were washed in the blood of the Lamb" (*DCA* 31). Faulkner's Reverend Shegog returns to this scriptural text when he repeats, "I got de ricklickshun en de blood of de Lamb!" at the end of *The Sound and the Fury* (295). In *Death Comes for the Archbishop*, the young Bishop "smiled at his mixed theology," as readers have sometimes smiled at Shegog's. But these characters mix their theology the same way, to establish the same theological point: goats can be washed clean in the blood of the Lamb.

Cather's third chapter begins in "late afternoon of Christmas Day" (32), about the same hour as the first reference to Christmas in Benjy's section of *The Sound and the Fury* (4–5). After Cather's description of Latour's study, we meet Father Vaillant, the accomplished cook. Just as Latour's study suggests the ground around Dilsey's cabin, Cather's description of Vaillant is curiously prophetic of Dilsey herself:

> Crimson from standing over an open fire, his rugged face was even homelier than usual — though one of the first things a stranger decided upon meeting Father Joseph was that the Lord had made few uglier men. He was short, skinny, bow-legged . . . and his countenance had little to recommend it but kindliness and vivacity. He looked old, though he was then about forty. His skin was hardened and seamed by exposure to weather in a bitter climate, his neck scrawny and wrinkled

like an old man's. A bold, blunt-tipped nose, positive chin, a very large mouth,—the lips thick and succulent but never loose, never relaxed, always stiffened by effort or working with excitement. (DCA 37–38)

The point, it should go without saying, is not that Faulkner needed lines from Cather before him in order to describe Dilsey, but rather that he deliberately appropriated the lines he noticed, with disguising gender change for camouflage, in order to create a competing version of a Christlike servant of man. He correctly assumed that only Cather would notice, and that noticing would make her smart, as in *feel a blow*. Both Dilsey and Vaillant, while occasionally agonizing over the simultaneous and also conflicting demands that pull at them, never seem to be lost in space or time; only their contrasting characters do that.

What particularly reminds one of Dilsey are Vaillant's mottoes: "Rest in action" (DCA 36); "Establish order at home" (40); "Serve Her in action" (41). The third motto even suggests many of the ironies Faulkner develops on the subject of virginity and Mrs. Compson's corruptions of the idea (Weinstein 430–42). Vaillant, like Dilsey, identifies with the poor and simple—those "least of these" that Faulkner usually builds his Christ images on. Further, Vaillant is especially receptive to miracles: "Doctrine is well enough for the wise, Jean; but the miracle is something we can hold in our hands and love" (DCA 50). When Dilsey arrives at her Easter service, with its Christmas bell over the pulpit and its orator preaching mixed theology on Latour's text, she experiences a miracle. She sees the first and the last, the beginning and the ending, with human wholeness that includes inevitable loss and death, bringing tears to her eyes.

And now we may be ready to ask *why*: *why* did Faulkner's eye focus so unblinkingly on that new novel *Death Comes for the Archbishop*, when all his energies were needed to produce his own stunning miracle and intended masterpiece in his novel to be? The apparent hook for him may have been that in *Death Comes for the Archbishop*, Cather once again deliberately and with provocation aforethought embedded a third identifiable sketch of William Faulkner, now costumed as Kit Carson. This is how he looks:

> This Carson . . . was very slight in frame, modest in manner, and he spoke English with a soft Southern drawl. His face was both thoughtful and alert: anxiety had drawn a permanent ridge between his blue eyes. Under his blond moustache his mouth had a singular refinement. The lips were full and delicately modeled. There was something curiously unconscious about his mouth, reflective, a little melancholy, —and something that suggested a capacity for tenderness. The Bishop felt a quick glow of pleasure in looking at the man. As he stood there in his buckskin clothes one felt in his standards, loyalties, a code which is not easily put into words but which is instantly felt when two men who live by it come together by chance. (DCA 75)

Carson responds in this meeting, "I'm right shy sir, and I'm always afraid of being disappointed. But I guess it will be all right from now on" (75). Most interesting is the fact that the sketched Carson has had no schooling because "he had got ahead of books, gone where the printing-press could not follow him" while preserving "a clean sense of honour and a compassionate heart" (DCA 76–77).

In connection with this Kit Carson in Cather's fiction, however, Faulkner might have seen and understood other ironies. Fictionalized Carson's life is a mixed bag: it was he "who finally subdued the last unconquered remnant of [the Navajos] in Canyon de Chelly" (DCA 293). His hands are not clean. But neither are Archbishop Latour's. Faulkner would have seen and understood an irony implicit in aging Archbishop Latour's elder-day satisfactions: having lived "to see two great wrongs righted, . . . the end of black slavery, and . . . the Navajos restored to their own country" (DCA 292). Any southerner would know that slavery's wrongs were still not righted by 1927, when Cather's novel was published. Any American should know that wrongs perpetrated against Native Americans were still not righted, either.

By 1927 young William Faulkner had already included unapologetic racist customs in his fiction, in his first novels preceding the appearance of Yoknapatawpha County. Racism would be required for a realistic Yoknapatawpha setting in 1929, of course, when that county materialized in print. Yet Faulkner was still defending the anachronisms of Mississippi race relations[9] in mid-century, in response to Autherine Lucy and the University of Alabama desegregation (Parini 383).In his recent biography, Jay Parini has given us a liberal and discrimination-hating Faulkner. But even Parini prominently concedes Faulkner's famous mid-century announcement: "As long as there's a middle road, all right, I'll be on it. But if it came to fighting I'd fight for Mississippi against the United States, even if it meant going out into the street and shooting Negroes" (381).[10] The elements of ethnic or racial abuse associated with Kit Carson, tracking down Navajos, could sting a Mississippi prototype.

At the end of Death Comes for the Archbishop, Cather's Latour has judged obtusely, or unrealistically, as a man whose judgment has been blunted by age. He sentimentalizes nostalgically, in book 9, about seeing the erasure of continuing forms of social abuse. He is getting old. Cather, however, was likely making a sad point subtly, perhaps about social justice and institutional administrators. The main (and heroic) action of building a church culminates at the end of book 8, the penultimate book in which Latour is in strong possession of his full faculties.

Thus, Cather's great novel has not only two beginnings but also two endings. At the point of its first moving crescendo, Latour blesses the departing Vaillant and asks his blessing in turn, as they prepare separately to face the future. At this point they are still hopeful and not yet willing to "smooth out" the past. The impermanent moment is sacred, in spite of the fact that Latour's good friend Carson, as recognizable as Victor Morse once was, has *betrayed* Latour's clerical charges, the natives he trapped in Canyon de Chelly. A quarter century later, in the mid-1950s, Faulkner seems deliberately to follow his Carson prototype, in his willingness to do violence. He later blamed his moves on being drunk. When giving an interview, "he had been drinking steadily but not enough to prevent his making comments more desperate and provocative than any he had thus far uttered" (Blotner 2:1590). Soon thereafter he wrote in a letter, "I don't know why I thought then that drinking could help, but that's what I was doing, a lot of it" (Blotner 2:1591). The Carson mold of undercurrent and destructive violence compels both writers, as does Cather's shrewd insistence that no man, not even a lovable or heroic character, is flawless.

The work done so far on Cather's impact on *The Sound and the Fury* emphasizes parallels between Cather characters and Quentin Compson; Charlotte Goodman relates Quentin to Niel Herbert, for many good reasons, and Jo Ann Middleton connects him to Jim Burden and Mr. Shimerda.[11] What these scholars have aptly demonstrated is a deep affinity between the more sensitive or fastidious (as well as autobiographical) males Cather created and the surrogate Faulkner recognized in Quentin. Looking back, he didn't confess so much as brag that he was Quentin (Oates 76). It is no coincidence, then, that Quentin not only resembles Latour's friend Kit Carson in manners, drawl, worried eyes, and watchful nature; he also resembles a whole cluster of characters in *Death Comes for the Archbishop* who are associated with its major protagonist, the discriminating Jean Latour.

Latour's special friends are *all* identified with the good manners that singularly mark Quentin's social behavior. Eusabio the Navajo, for example, has "unfailing good manners" (DCA 232). He is further connected with "the Indian manner to vanish into the landscape" (233), as Quentin prepares to do as the sun goes down on the evening of his suicide. Don Antonio Olivares, the rich Mexican *ranchero*, is another. In his house "the French priests were always welcome and were most cordially entertained" (176). We are told, "Next to his old friend Manuel Chavez, the two French priests were the men in Santa Fé whose company he most enjoyed, and he let them see it. He was a man who cherished his friends" (178) — surely the essence of good manners.

The strongest parallels thus predictably exist between Quentin Compson and Jean Latour. Latour's head "was built for the seat of a fine intelligence. His brow was open, generous, reflective, his features handsome and somewhat severe. There was a singular elegance about the hands," while "everything showed him to be a man of gentle birth — brave, sensitive, courteous. His manners, even when he was alone in the desert, were distinguished. He had a kind of courtesy" (DCA 19). Quentin's courtesy wins everyone from Mrs. Bland to Julio's little sister. Conversely, when Faulkner writes to show testy annoyance, he will stress fictional ruptures of courtesy and good manners. Almost immediately he turns Burdens into Bundrens to make this point seven ways.

Upon occasion, Latour, like Quentin, finds that "disorder was almost more than his fastidious taste could bear" (DCA 144); Quentin spends his first moments packing his belongings and his last moments making sure his room is neat and the bloodstains removed from the new suit he leaves behind for the Deacon. While Latour suffers "seizures of vertigo" under severe stress (DCA 20), Quentin faints when confronting Dalton Ames and apparently blacks out when fighting Gerald Bland. Latour "could not form new ties" (DCA 253), and Quentin spends his last day of life mourning his family and trying to evade his Harvard acquaintances. Thus, Latour suffers, as Quentin does too, when he lies "unable to sleep, with the sense of failure clutching at his heart. . . . His soul had become a barren field. He had nothing within himself to give. . . . His work seemed superficial, a house built upon the sands" (DCA 211). To speak in understatement, Quentin's soul also seems a barren field and his home seems built upon the metaphoric sands. Faulkner sadistically gives to Latour's creator the ultimate melancholic December night Christmas present in *Light in August*, opposite that which Latour receives from Old Sada.

Toward the beginning of *Death Comes for the Archbishop*, Latour, just returned from Mexico, hears a "bell with beautiful tone" (43). He later makes guesses about the metal that could produce a sound in which "each note floated through the air like a globe of silver" (43), and speculates that "the silver of the Spaniards was really Moorish, was it not?" (44–45). Toward the beginning of Quentin's section in *The Sound and the Fury*, we read, "The hour began to strike. . . . It was awhile before the last stroke ceased vibrating. It stayed in the air, more felt than heard [like the overtones divined but not heard by the ear in Cather's "The Novel Démeublé," published in 1922], for a long time. Like all the bells that ever rang still ringing in the long dying light rays and Jesus and St. Francis talking about his sister" (SF 79). To Latour's association of the bell with a mixed history, Vaillant replies petulantly, "What are you doing Jean? Trying to make my bell out an infidel?" When Latour defends his guesswork, "Father Vaillant sniffed. 'I noticed that scholars always manage to dig out something belittling'" (45). Faulkner himself might sniff, in turn, "You ain't seen nothing yet!"

A brilliant writer must first be a brilliant reader. The comparisons being made here between *Death Comes for the Archbishop* and *The Sound and the Fury* highlight the strength of these readers' minds and the inventiveness of their busy pencils. Faulkner decided not just to enter the literary mainstream where Cather already swam but to enter with a successful plunge indicating he knew how to reach its central channel. He was after gold medals and willing to work unceasingly for them. But what surprises me most at this point is how quickly Faulkner metamorphoses into the genius we recognize. Cather's renditions of him must have cheered as well as goaded him. As we will notice in the next chapter, it was now Cather's turn to squirm, to become more than amply annoyed when she noticed how her material looked, successfully manhandled by Bill Faulkner. Her prophetic line from *My Ántonia* now on her tombstone may have come to haunt her in her lifetime: "That is happiness; to be dissolved into something complete and great. When it comes to one, it comes as naturally as sleep" (MA 18). She may have come to register wryly that that line was written before she read of Yoknapatawpha.

5

Dust Tracks on Some Roads

WHAT HAPPENED BETWEEN Willa Cather and William Faulkner in the years 1930 to 1932 seems uncanny, as well as disturbing, even if we start (stretching credulity) by positing the possibility that by this time they are both able to anticipate the moves or thoughts of the other, to respond in their preferred ways, and then to leave a sense of inflicted injury behind. Such intuitions can, of course, happen. Recently, novelist John Irving told a *New York Times* interviewer of discovering the life story of his deceased biological father by mentioning on television his own actual birth name, instead of the stepfather's name he has used professionally. Eventually a half brother called by his own first given name got in contact and told Irving of their father's last years. The arresting fact, however, was that Irving had already imagined and written that story with uncanny accuracy, and had used it as the end of his most recent novel.[1] Uncanny things happen, even when factual or logical explanations can't be found for them.

In any case, in the years between 1930 and 1932, both Cather and Faulkner were writing masterpieces and tours de force: Faulkner in *As I Lay Dying* (1930) and *Light in August* (1932); Cather in *Shadows on the Rock* (1931) and *Obscure Destinies* (1932). The *textual* evidence, in contrast to the "known facts," might suggest that each was responding directly to works of the other: *As I Lay Dying* seems a corrective to "Neighbour Rosicky"; the second two stories in *Obscure Destinies* then seem to answer and rebut *As I Lay Dying*; and *Light in August* arrives as an intended annihilator in response to *Obscure Destinies*. The publication information, however, *seems*—on the face of it—to make those assumptions impossible. This chapter merely presents, therefore, textual parallels in the works of these two writers, which are arresting and seem to form a bridge in the air, like Dickinson's crescent in the sea, ungrounded by certainty.

One views these texts with increasing perplexity. For example, textual evidence we'll now review provokes a suspicion that it was not her several novels but rather the short story "Neighbour Rosicky" that excited Faulkner's sharp derision, which he then expressed in *As I Lay Dying*. *Textual* evidence suggests that an indignant Cather swatted back at him, intending to hit him where he lived, in "Two Friends," and then swung in left-right-punch style decisively in the masterful "Old Mrs. Harris." The *text* of *Light in August* suggests that Faulkner decided he had had enough; he was now ready to end the contest as well as her, for good measure. He constructed a parodic caricature of Willa Cather, used the name Joanna Burden (referencing her autobiographical Jim Burden), and slit her throat: Merry (Joe) Christmas. But barring gossipy literary agents who would leak to each other, the presently provable facts do not support this textual fox trot.

It presently appears that Faulkner couldn't have seen the story "Neighbour Rosicky" before he wrote a detailed devastation of it. And he couldn't have read Cather's counterattacks before completing *Light in August*. On the other hand, the denial is as hard to defend as the argument, for the fact is that every one of Cather's descriptive phrases for the entitled subject in "Neighbour Rosicky"—which is set in Nebraska farming country instead of the other places this title character has lived, such as Bohemia, London, and New York—is specifically or explicitly countered, denied, or inverted in Faulkner's novel, down to the metaphors. Ostensibly, thereafter, when she included that lead story among the three great master stories of *Obscure Destinies*, she patronizingly shrugged off his derisive view of it. His imaginably indignant response to her three intentionally emasculating stories is symbolic rape and murder, as Joe Christmas slashes back.

Faulkner's first imaginable engine of attack on Cather's 1928 story is the character of Anse Bundren of rural Mississippi in *As I Lay Dying*. "A myriad" of details invert each other in portraits of the two farmers, Anse Bundren and Anton Rosicky. How that could happen is a sticking mystery. But *why* Cather would assume the novel was deliberately malicious is not hard to see. And *why* Faulkner would feel her response was worse than malicious is not mysterious either.

First the "known facts" about "Neighbour Rosicky." Cather end-signs this story, the first of the three tales collected in *Obscure Destinies*, "New York, 1928." Woodress explains that the story was especially close to her heart because it was written after her father died, in a year when she wrote almost nothing else. Not much else may have seemed worth writing, but the character *is* another version of Cuzak, from Faulkner's favorite *My Ántonia*. It therefore *does* take another look at that novel's second family of man, sprung from Ántonia, the founder of races, but from a male point of view. At the least, "Neighbour Rosicky" celebrates a good man, a good marriage, and a "complete and beautiful" life, either the kind she might have wished for her father or the kind Faulkner had ignored in his earliest fictions. She may have wished to insist not only that the good life was imaginable but also that an account of it was possible to write and market. "Neighbour Rosicky" is certainly the opposite of a tale told by an idiot, and it signifies a great deal.

The story depicts the man who married Annie Sadilek, the prototype for Ántonia. Ántonia's story, as we have seen, gripped Faulkner's imagination most forcibly. This story jerks back what he remade of it in 1929, in *The Sound and the Fury*. Both writers from this point on appear to know not only what they are doing but also what the other is doing. Cather, however, leaves deliberate footprints under Faulkner's windows. Astonishingly, on the inside flap copy of the dust cover for the *1933 edition* of Cather's *April Twilights* (of all bizarre places), we read, "In *Neighbour Rosicky* admirers of *My Ántonia* will discover a story that is almost like a pendant to that remarkable book (which is much more popular today than when it was first published fifteen years ago)." Metaphoric language noted. *April Twilights*, as we have seen, is also a title William Faulkner considered truncating as "Twilight," his first title for *The Sound and the Fury*.

"Neighbour Rosicky" is the story of a man who stands up to die. It is possible to see a parodic version of the fact in the title *As I Lay Dying*. It is also the portrait of a man with a gift for loving well. As the latter, it could almost serve as a moral *fable*. (William Faulkner's *A Fable*, a book he seemed to work longest on and sometimes think his most important, wasn't published until 1954.) "Neighbour Rosicky" was serialized in *Woman's Home Companion* in April and May of 1930, nearly a quarter century earlier than Faulkner's *A Fable*, and then was collected in *Obscure Destinies* in August of 1932. Thus, though it was clearly written in 1928, and was in her agent's hands before 1929 when Faulkner began writing *As I Lay Dying*, there is still no easily apparent way—short of agent transgression—that Faulkner could have seen, heard about, or read it before he finished his next great book.

Faulkner's physical activities in this period become relevant here. According to Blotner, he was in New York in the autumn of 1928 (about the time Cather presumably finished polishing Rosicky) to sell stories and to help with the job of cutting *Flags in the Dust* down to *Sartoris*. New York, of course, is a big town. Faulkner was again living mostly with friends in Greenwich Village, again near Washington Square. Cather at this point had been forced to vacate her Bank Street apartment, and was camped (for several years) at the Grosvenor Hotel, a short skip and hop from the Washington Square Arch. While Faulkner was in New York this time he was often entertaining guests with his stories: "When guests dropped in during the evening [in a stretch when he was staying with Jim Devine and Leon Scales "upstate" at 111 Street], he would take off his shoes and tell stories, that made him the center of attention—about his Mississippi youth and his Canadian service" (Blotner 229).

Back in Greenwich Village on Vandam Street, Faulkner and his artist roommate frequently went to literary salons in the neighborhood, to get the ample sandwiches, good liquor, and human company. Blotner explains, "Faulkner would be something of a celebrity, with two novels and a book of poems in print, another soon to be published, and still another being read at a publisher's" (230). As Blotner stresses the Faulkner routines, "Again, Faulkner would sit on the floor, cross-legged, his shoes beside him, telling some of his stories. . . . [And the two roommates] would take long walks to places where the famous had lived" (230). When it comes to passing good stories around literary circles, of course, New York is one of the smallest towns on earth. In any case, Faulkner submitted a story entitled "As I Lay Dying" to Alfred Dashiell at *Scribner's* in November of 1928 (Blotner 231), and that's a fact Cather could easily have heard about, as she could have heard some of his stories from neighborhood literary gossips like Viola Roseboro. She could also have rather easily guessed that *As I Lay Dying* was meant to be a take-off, or rip-off, of *Death Comes for the Archbishop*, certainly including that Carson portrait of a southern illiterate, over which conscience might pinch.

The novel *As I Lay Dying*, according to Dianne Cox, was begun, and dated, October 25, 1929, and then typed, with the typescript dated January 12, 1930. While it was not published until October 6, 1930, after the magazine publication of "Neighbour Rosicky," the novel's absolutely pervasive pattern nevertheless re-

verses and alters the character of Cather's paterfamilias by invert-
ing every Catherian phrase and feature. The fact seems preter-
naturally coincidental. In any case, the differences between these
two poor farmers created by Cather and Faulkner are essential to
the designs of these two fictions. Charles A. Peek highlights the
difference when he summarizes *As I Lay Dying*, "Hence, the novel
could be seen to constitute a critique of frontier values and the
American myths . . . that drove westward expansion (Hamblin
and Peek 22). Peek adds of the Bundrens, "Their failure to either
alter or escape their world is an indictment of many of our cherished myths: work ethic and action, women's roles, reason, and
sensitivity" (23). Kathleen Svendsen suggests further that Anse
is an "ans-wer" to Anton.

Unless we count *Sanctuary* because of its corncobs (a work
written between January and May of 1929 but not published till
1931), *As I Lay Dying* can qualify as Faulkner's *first* clearly intended thumb of the nose at his perceived caricaturist, written
in his most self-consciously ambitious style. Cox reminds us that
Faulkner wrote to Hal Smith as he began his intended tour de
force, "Name of the new novel is 'As I Lay Dying'. How's that for
high?" (xiv). And would not a reference to approaching death
qualify as *high*, after Cather's recent similar title? High- or lowlife, Cather seems to have felt that the tour de force novel was
hostile to her and her work.

One Cather response may have been *Shadows on the Rock*
(1931). That novel, set in seventeenth-century Quebec (where life
would be a lot harder and colder than rural Mississippi), features
matrifocal society in which all enduring heroes, survivors, and
continuously contributing shapers are female. It also centers on
a resolutely good-girl heroine who knows who she is and where
she wants to be from beginning to end. Its author demonstrates
that she can deliberately manufacture fictional history for or from
the past as well as anybody, and from the first sentence at that.[2]
It could be intended as a thunderous retort to Faulkner's "two

lost ladies" of *The Sound and the Fury*. But the more interesting
Cather response seems to me to be found in the two final stories
of *Obscure Destinies* (1932), "Old Mrs. Harris" and "Two Friends."
The last came first.

"Two Friends" concludes *Obscure Destinies*, and was first serialized in July, only a month before the book's *August* publication.
"Old Mrs. Harris," the volume's middle story, did not appear in a
magazine form until *after* the book had appeared, in September
through November of 1932. One might ask why the book wasn't
held until after the magazine publication, and the chance to ad-
vertise for the anticipated "Christmas trade" is one answer. The
postpublication serialization, on the other hand, seems a real
gamble, at least from the magazine perspective. Still, we assume
both worked to accelerate all sales. The collection's three stories
are all tours de force of different kinds, even to an unsophisti-
cated eye. "Two Friends," we might add, was end-dated *Pasadena,
1931*. Cather was in Pasadena just before her mother's death in
1931. Pointedly, the story is deliberately associated with the year
in which Cather's Cécile also appeared, as if it were almost a sequel to *Shadows on the Rock*. A hostile eye might regard both as
reprimands for cynicism. In fact, Pasadena becomes the setting
Faulkner uses a bit later for his malevolent story "The Golden
Land" (1935). Faulkner's story is about the degenerate family of
a feeble Nebraska mother who wants only to go back home to a
place (like Catherton) that is named for her husband's Nebraska
family.[3]

This literary air seems full of mischief by August of 1932, when
Obscure Destinies arrived on the market. So it is not so startling that *Light in August* is published October 6 of 1932 as well.
Faulkner's title, to stress the obvious, follows the August publications of both *Shadows on the Rock* (1931) and *Obscure Destinies*
(1932). Parsing these moves is the task at hand. We acknowledge
that if Cather's agent, the great Paul Reynolds, mentioned her
1928 story "Neighbour Rosicky" during any New York power

lunches or encounters he may have shared with Faulkner's agent Ben Wasson, Wasson at this time had in hand a story named "As I Lay Dying" to report.

Our first job at this point is simply to recognize the startlingly coincidental contrasts between Anton Rosicky and Anse Bundren. They begin in Cather's first sentence, when a concerned Dr. Burleigh tells Rosicky he has a "bad heart" and Rosicky protests. First, the homophone *burly* suggests the size of Faulkner's Doc Peabody, soon to appear at Addie Bundren's bedside. Second, the question of what is a good heart or a bad heart dominates these works. Third, our paired works exist to explore forms of protest.

Anse Bundren, like Anton Rosicky, has a plot-driving health problem: he can't sweat (as Anton is also forbidden to do). Instead, Anse uses his energy to protest his sons' attempts to labor for any profit but his own—as, for example, when Jewel clears a field to buy a horse. Anton, conversely, injures his heart irreparably while surreptitiously trying to clear thistles from his son Rudolph's alfalfa field. Sick Ros[e]-icky's old heart is tired from a lifetime of hard and generous labor (see Skaggs, "Cather's Complex Tale"). While all Bundrens may have bad hearts of one kind or another, Anse seems most heartless of all. He more than the rest of his "care-kin" seems heartless to the others' needs or desires, while Rosicky has "a special gift for loving people" (66).

Rosicky's physical characteristics force startling contrasts. His triangular eyes seem made for measuring others accurately, that is, for triangulating. All Bundrens have notably defining eyes, but Faulkner's descriptions are negative: Anse's eyes, for example, are "like burnt out cinders" (31). Cather's Anton "was shorter and broader than when [his wife Mary] married him; his back had grown broad and curved, a good deal like the shell of an old turtle, and his arms and legs were short" (NR 31). Anse's inept movements also suggest an old turtle, and his back is also humped, a feature mentioned almost immediately (AILD 16), while his arms hang out as a turtle's forelimbs: "Anse's wrists dangle out of his sleeves: I never see him with a shirt on that looked like it was his in all my life" (30). While Anton enjoys patching his family clothes because he was trained as a tailor, the slick serge patch *inappropriately* sewn on Anse's overalls somehow makes the overalls disreputable (28). Anse's brogans, placed beside his feet, "look as though they had been hacked with a blunt ax out of pig iron" (11). Anton, conversely, provides himself and his family with luxurious physical comforts, even though they don't always "get ahead" (NR 50). In each presenting feature, in short, the two suggest opposites symmetrically arranged to balance by contrast.

Their internal characters and philosophies are even more startlingly counterbalanced: Anton "was a very simple man. He was like a tree that has not many roots, yet one tap root that goes down deep" (32). One tap root makes Rosicky seem to represent "deep" or stable values. The tree metaphor, famously essential to Anse, makes Faulkner's farmer seem foolish: "The Lord put roads for traveling: why He laid them down flat on the earth. When He aims for something to be always a-moving He makes it longways, like a road or a horse or a wagon, but when he aims for something to stay put, He makes it up-and-down ways, like a tree or a man. . . . He aimed for . . . [men] to stay put like a tree or a stand of corn" (AILD 35). Of course, Anton Rosicky, who is compared to a tree with one tap root, has paradoxically traveled from Bohemia to London to New York to Nebraska. But Anse, who prefers immobility and "has not been in town in twelve years" (41), takes to the road when he needs new teeth and a wife.

That fact brings up the essential contrast in these two fictions: the matter of family relations. Even his doctor can see that Cather's Rosicky is that rare and lucky man who can take comfort in his sons; Dr. Burleigh advises the patient to stay home and enjoy them. Anse Bundren stays home—is first seen sitting on his porch dipping snuff and barefoot—but never stops whining about his bad luck and bad sons, though they, as the Rosicky boys also, try to do his work for him. They simply provide no comfort that Anse values.

Anton's wife, Mary, finds, "It is hard to see any one who has become like your own body to you" (NR 23), and is proud to recall that her husband "had never touched her without gentleness" because "there wasn't anything brutal in the short, broadbacked man" (24). Conversely, Faulkner's Doc Peabody is so sure that Addie is one of those farm wives "clinging to some trifling animal to whom they never were more than pack-horses" (AILD 44), that he makes sure not to arrive at her bedside until he's confident Anse "has wore her out at last. And a damn good thing. . . . I knew that if it had finally occurred to Anse himself that he needed . . . [a doctor], it was already too late" (40–41). That other doctor, Burleigh of Nebraska, will drive eight miles in winter to get to the warm, friendly, jolly, happy Rosicky family kitchen for an ample breakfast; Doc Peabody of Mississippi complains bitterly about the skimpy and unappetizing cold greens offered at the Bundren house for supper.

We can read not only Anse's philosophy but also Rosicky's: "What Rosicky really hoped for his boys was that they could get through the world without ever knowing much about the cruelty of human beings. 'Their mother and me ain't prepared them for that,' he sometimes said to himself. . . . In all these years [on his farm], he had never had to take a cent from anyone in bitter need,—never had to look at the face of a woman become like a wolf's from struggle and famine" (NR 61). In contrast, no naturalist could want more lessons in human cruelty than Faulkner's Bundrens provide each other. Anse takes money from his children with no compunction and looks at his wife's and daughter's desperate faces with no comprehension. Rosicky, his mirror opposite, affirms farming: "You didn't have to choose between bosses and strikers, and go wrong either way. You didn't have to do with dishonest and cruel people. They were the only things in his experience he had found terrifying and horrible; the look in the eyes of a dishonest and crafty man, of a scheming and rapacious woman" (59).

William Faulkner seems almost to have underlined all these negative phrases from "Neighbour Rosicky," to make sure he included them in his Bundren family. The clan is headed by a dishonest and crafty father, watched by a scheming and rapacious neighbor, Cora Tull, and divided into the bosses and the would-be strikers, all of whom—with possibly the exception of boss Anse—lose whatever they most value. The Rosickys seem admirable; the Bundrens seem clownish. Each work presents a view of the world. Whatever Faulkner intended, Cather seems to have taken offense and taken it personally. Her reply was "Two Friends." What she did there was to tell one of Bill Faulkner's best family stories first, with instructions to him about how he should write his chosen material, and with resounding moral conclusions appended. It reads like a moral fable. Faulkner "would say that as an artist, he felt he could create better characters than God could" (Blotner 216). Cather says in this story that she could create better characters out of his most familiar family materials than Faulkner could. That intimation had to goad, as she had to intend that it would. A reduced version of the story in question is in Blotner's one-volume biography:

> The Colonel had been doing business there [in the First National Bank of Oxford] in the same way during the ten years since its founding. He would sit in his office at the rear before his big, cluttered roll-top cherry desk, but often he would conduct bank business at a desk out front. The Colonel was there every day. . . .
>
> Joe Parks and several others had carefully worked out a plan. After the reading of the annual report, they broke it to the Colonel. They wanted him to resign as president. The old man reacted with shock and outrage . . . and Joe Parks was elected president of John Wesley Thompson Falkner's bank.

When the Colonel cooled down he did what he could to put the best possible face on things — but he brooded over his eviction. One day not long afterward, as he sat with a crony in a cane-bottom chair tilted against the front of the bank, his resentment exploded into action. He went to Relbue Price's hardware store for two tin buckets and then strode across the square and opened an account at the Bank of Oxford. He retained some of his stock, but he would not deal with the bank which had repudiated him. (86)

"Two Friends" constitutes theft of a prize Faulkner family story known all over Oxford. Faulkner won't forget this plundering, and he'll return her bank references in *The Reivers*.

The details that are shared in the two bank stories — Blotner's and Cather's — are interesting. The key incident is the angry transfer of funds from the bank of a former friend to the rival bank across the street. Silas Garber's bank in Red Cloud was called the Farmers' and Merchants' Bank (in which building the Willa Cather Pioneer Memorial was once housed);[4] the analogous name Faulkner later locates in Jefferson is the Merchants and Farmers Bank, and it shows he knows exactly what he is doing.

We can also spot smaller details that make both stories live. For example, the pillar-of-town-society businessmen of Cather's title "had been friends for ten years before I knew them" (196); ten years is the number the Young Colonel had been president of his bank and had been conducting business activities in tones audible to others, as expansive sidewalk conversation would have been in either hometown. The Colonel's folksy manner corresponds to that by which Cather's R. E. Dillon (of semaphore initials) "learned all he needed to know about how much money it was safe to advance a farmer who wanted to feed cattle, or to buy a steam thrasher or build a new barn" (TF 198). Blotner's cane-bottom chair is another specific parallel: "Every evening when he came back to the store after supper, Dillon had one of his clerks bring two arm-chairs out to the wide sidewalk that ran beside the red brick wall, — office chairs of the old-fashioned sort, with a low round back which formed a half-circle to enclose the sitter, and spreading legs, the front ones slightly higher" (203). Blotner's "cherry roll-top desk" where the Colonel could be found every day recalls Cather's assertions that Dillon "and his store were one" (198), and that "he was there to be called on" (203); in winter he could be found with Trueman "playing checkers in the office behind the wire screening" (199). The anger and outrage prompting Oxford's Colonel to transfer his assets is parsed in Cather: "To change your bank was one of the most final things you could do. The little, unsuccessful men were pleased, as they always are at the destruction of anything strong and fine" (224).

What strikes me about these details of background and setting, however, is that they are *amplified* in Cather, who usually advocates selecting and culling. Cather seems to be *filling in* a story, the same one that exists (well told later), with an emphasis on plot, in Blotner's biography. Blotner's story, studied as if it were a fiction, emphasizes the ostensible theme in *Obscure Destinies*. Yet only at first glance is that theme a rupturing friendship. The more important "moral" is that the rupture did not need to happen, was wasteful and useless. A third and perhaps most important theme in Cather's story is the lasting effect on the narrating observer who tells this tale.

It also seems noteworthy that R. E. Dillon, Cather's Nebraska banker, is described as if he were a modernist or cubist "planes in relation," or experimentalist, artwork: "His skin was very white, bluish on his shaven cheeks and chin. Shaving must have been a difficult process for him, because there were no smooth expanses for the razor to glide over. The bony structure of his face was prominent and unusual; high cheek-bones, a bold Roman nose, a chin cut by deep lines, with a hard dimple at the tip, a jutting ridge over his eyes where his curly black eyebrows grew and met. It was a face in many planes, as if the carver had whittled and modeled and indented to see how far he could go" (194–95). J. H. Trueman, the Young Colonel figure who does the funds transfer, "was fully ten years older than Dillon, — in his early fifties, when I knew him; large, heavy, very slow in his movements, not given to exercise. His countenance was as unmistakably American as Dillon's was not, — but American of that period, not of this" (196): more a John Singer Sergeant portrait, perhaps, say of Henry James.

Cather could have heard this story secondhand and fleshed it out in her characteristic manner, using Red Cloud locations with which she was familiar, and Dillon's R.E.D. initials, reminding of a Red Cloud site, democratic politics, or drawing blood, as her signature flourish. But her tone of wide-eyed innocence, or of sad and wise regret, camouflages a two-pronged frontal attack. The first purpose of this invasion of Yoknapatawpha material, I surmise, is to address Faulkner directly, but in a manner only he can hear. The style she adopts does the trick. The second is to talk about betrayals, using the title of a story from Cervantes, "The Story of the Two Friends," about a man who perversely enlists his best friend to test his wife's fidelity. When two friends test each other so intimately, all lose, or to put it in the vernacular, everybody gets screwed (*Don Quixote*, pt. 1, chs. 33–34).

The lecturing or hectoring starts at Cather's "Two Friends" opening. By 1932 both Cather and Faulkner have proved they can write brilliantly compressed first sentences (Faulkner has done it four times in *The Sound and the Fury* alone). In those opening sentences, reinforced by the subsequent first paragraph, all the important matters of the story to come are implied or defined. Furthermore, one might add, both by now have mastered the device of multiple openings. But what Cather's *short* story does is to show that the device can serve in a compressed, short fiction (not long novel) form: In "Two Friends," one paragraph composed of four sentences flicks a whiplash at Faulkner four different ways before the story starts again.

The second paragraph uses a fairy-tale, once-upon-a-time, this-is-just-a-child's-tale throwaway beginning: "Long ago, before the invention of the motorcar (which has made more changes in the world than the War, which indeed produced the particular kind of war that happened just a hundred years after Waterloo), in a little wooden town in a shallow Kansas river valley, there lived two friends" (194). We see in this second beginning the subject defined—two friends—at the end of the first sentence. That (second) first sentence starts the narrative action. But we also recognize that Faulkneresque parenthetical digression that widens the story's resonance in time. Further, we identify two subjects Faulkner loved and made his own—the automobile and war. He'll stress a car and warlike combat or competition in his last work, *The Reivers*, when he turns his entire attention to Willa Cather. But parody, it appears, is a talent they share.

Before this action will begin, however, the first paragraph of "Two Friends" arrests attention (as the prologue of *Death Comes for the Archbishop* recently did). The first sentence reads, "Even in early youth, when the mind is so eager for the new and untried, while it is still a stranger to faltering and fear, we yet like to think that there are certain unalterable realities somewhere at the bottom of things." Unalterable realities is what youthful Quentin longs for in *The Sound and the Fury* before he "hits bottom." As current readers, we note that the one of ours, the *we-spokesman* here who is also the voice of a village, is a voice Faulkner used in "A Rose for Emily" and found a model for in *A Lost Lady*. We also see a piously forgiving look back at foolish, typical youth, an implied nurturing of youthful callowness or callousness by one who maturely recalls the story now to be told; it's very patronizing. We spot the stresses on "new and untried" and on the naiveté of trying to remain "a stranger to faltering and fear," not to mention old verities dredged from murky memories—all securely assessed from an older and wiser point of view. That perspective might be infuriating.

The story's second sentence identifies the materials out of which stories are made, whether one's own stories or another's: "These anchors may be ideas; but more often they are merely pictures, vivid memories, which in some unaccountable and very personal way give us courage." At this point we may recall all the comments stressing pictures and memories with which Faulkner explained the origins of *The Sound and the Fury*—the little girl's dirty drawers seen in a tree, his identification with Quentin. One also flags that Faulknerian measure of virtue—courage. We must always wonder whether Faulkner chose to validate Cather's facts (as in the Sartoris materials) by restating them, or just chose to reclaim what he felt was his own, as he might repossess Cather's more speculative statements: for example, that one creates mainly from pictures and memories that give one courage. Did he choose to adopt her postures or did he prefer to repossess by reclaiming her thefts? Whichever it was, "Two Friends" now moves to a daring and provocative sentence that, for its length, grammatical complexity, and parallel cadences, plus its fanciful metaphors, sounds far more like Faulkner than Cather: "The seagulls, that seem so much creatures of the free wind and waves, that are as homeless as the sea (able to rest upon the tides and ride the storm, needing nothing but water and sky), at certain seasons even they go back to something they have known before; to remote islands and lonely ledges that are their breeding grounds" (193–94). This first paragraph ends with a sentence that might sound to a younger writer like archly superior Aunt Willa: "The restlessness of youth has such retreats, even though it may be ashamed of them." The offenses of this sentence, however, might include its equating a restless youth with a flighty and birdbrained seagull—"gulled," in fact, by its nature. Gulling then brings us back to the title, as Cervantes once used it.

Once these striking sentences get "Two Friends" going, the character who serves as the Colonel equivalent, J. H. Trueman, is presented so approvingly, from his name to his character to his habits, that nobody would accuse either narrator or writer of malice. The only one who might object to such admiring piety might be the one who wanted to tell about the character in a different tone—as, for example, Faulkner used with curmudgeonly Banker Bayard Sartoris, also modeled on the Colonel. In any case, the presentation of J. H. Trueman, starting with the spelling of his underscored name, is so clearly approving that it amounts to an implied preference, as well as a wide-eyed "Who, me?" to the imagined accusations of the character's indignant heir.

Sooner or later we catch the provocative note here. Cather's most famous critical essay, "The Novel Démeublé," has been asking since 1922, "But are the banking system and the Stock Exchange worth being written about at all?" (*NUF* 46). When she allows a "cattleman" to represent the Stock Exchange (thereby acknowledging the chicanery which actually named the place and practices in lower Manhattan), and then juxtaposes that character with a banker, she forces the scholar-reader to ask what worthwhile thing, or real thing, the story is meant to be about. The first answer she forces is "ruptured friendship."

Trueman's character is patrician: "For any form of pushing or boosting he had a cold, unqualified contempt." Did Cather perhaps feel pushed around about this time? The appearance of Trueman is also useful: "All this was in his face, —heavy, immobile, rather melancholy, not remarkable in any particular. But the moment one looked at him one felt solidity, an entire absence of anything mean or small, easy carelessness, courage, a high sense of honour" (196). He and his friend R. E. Dillon seem "solid and well-built," "secure and established" (197), and "represented success and power" (194). They are the only men in town who wear silk shirts, and "they stood with easy assurance on a deck that was their own" (198). One could not, in fact, easily object to such portraits unless one were perceived as essentially different from either—a Count No Count, as William Faulkner was once nicknamed.

The main trick of the story, or the tricky part, concerns the narrator. The voice that remembers the two friends emerges from a most curious creation: a genderless child who looks back from a distance. Now the setting of a brick wall against which chairs can tip and which is a short distance from "home" matches exactly the view from the first Cather home in Red Cloud, two blocks from North Webster, the main street. Thus, most readers have equated the child with Willa. Further, R. E. Dillon seems modeled after Mr. Miner (the store owner on whom Mr. Harling is also modeled in *My Ántonia*). Thus, because the tone of the story is full of pathos and nostalgia, many assume Cather is constructing another "autobiographical" story here.

In fact, the absence of any pronoun indicating the sex of the child in question is both singular and arresting. The only reason to assume the child is female, much less Cather herself, is that the narrative voice for this symbolically named town of Singleton[5] is a child who says, "The road, just in front of the sidewalk where I sat and played jacks, would be ankle-deep in dust, and seemed to drink up the moonlight like folds of velvet. It drank up sound, too; muffled the wagon-wheels and hoof-beats; lay soft and meek like the last residuum of material things, — the soft bottom resting-place. Nothing in the world, not snow mountains or blue seas, is so beautiful in moonlight as the soft, dry summer roads in a farming country, roads where the white dust falls back from the slow wagon-wheel" (211–12). In short, the setting is nostalgic, told through the unreliable memories of a child, about a generic country village with dusty summer roads. It is as likely a "poetic" description of Mississippi as of Nebraska, as Faulkner's almost countless country wagon scenes amply prove. Such a scene emerges in the opening sequences of *Light in August*, soon to follow. Further, the only potential gender indicator is the jacks, but a child playing *jacks* (usually considered a girl's game) can also symbolize a male of uncertain sexual identity, trying to learn maleness at the feet of his town's best representatives of masculine success and power.

Furthermore, all the other clues in this story suggest a male child. That child sits for hours on summer nights at the feet of his two models, without raising eyebrows. The child performs "countless errands that I was sent upon day and night" (197) without any apprehensiveness about personal danger. He is radically different from Thea Kronborg of *The Song of the Lark*, who alarms her siblings by attending one dance on the wrong side of town. The child of "Two Friends" hangs around Dillon's store and chats with all the (presumably male) clerks who work late at night, whenever they're not busy; which they apparently consider natural; and he is sent every night to the post office. He knows when the late secret poker games begin, and who attends them. Similarly, the child is allowed to hear the discussion about how Swedes treat their women, conducted without a glance his way. He also hears the two solid citizens joke of managing "to run this town with one fancy house instead of two" (214) without soliciting an apology or necessitating a shift in conversation, as a ten- to thirteen-year-old girl would surely do. In short, the narrator most resembles an early-adolescent male desperately trying to figure out how to grow up to be an acceptable man in an unlikely place. The Red Cloud–like setting is convenient camouflage. One subtext of this remarkable story involves establishing a viable male sexual identity against the odds, which include the occultation, or erasure, of Venus. The odds also include an inclination to do things many associate with girls—such as playing jacks, telling stories, and watching the stars. But that business about witnessing the disappearance of Venus could really hurt.

Cather's two friends allow their friendship to rupture over a political question, that is, over the question of *who will win*. That's the question Cather and Faulkner seem to square off over at this point. And the story suggests that such ruptures, provoking loss that affects everybody, would be unthinkable if one did not pursue that political question.

As do the other two stories in *Obscure Destinies*, "Two Friends" displays, beyond its tour de force beginnings, a stunning finale. The conclusion underscores that thing not named but felt on the page, which is truly created. It concerns William Faulkner:

> The breaking-up of that friendship . . . was a real loss to me, and has ever since been a regret. More than once, in Southern countries where there is a smell of dust and dryness in the air and the nights are intense, I have come upon a stretch of dusty white road drinking up the moonlight beside a blind wall, and have felt a sudden sadness. Perhaps it was not until the next morning that I knew why, — and then only because I had dreamed of Mr. Dillon or Mr. Trueman in my sleep. When that old scar is occasionally touched by chance, it rouses the old uneasiness; the feeling of something broken that could so easily have been mended; of something delightful that was senselessly wasted, of a truth that was accidentally distorted — one of the truths we want to keep.

6

Sparring

AT FIRST CATHER'S *Shadows on the Rock* (1931) seems only
to address a good girl named Cécile Auclair, who perpetuates a
satisfying way of life in Quebec at the end of the seventeenth century (see Skaggs, "Good Girl in Her Place"). Such a wholesome,
law-abiding, parent-honoring lass is never portrayed by Faulkner
at all, unless in a frigid and fearful coward such as Narcissa Benbow. I would pass over this fact, were it not for the excised fragment, now in the Drew University library, that Frederick B. Adams, once owner of the world's most important private Cather
collection, considered an alternate ending to the novel. Labeled
"Cécile," this fragment not only survived in Adams's hands but
has recently stirred controversy by being assessed differently by
two prominent scholars, John J. Murphy and Ann Romines.[1] Romines examines feminist issues that the excision raises about a
girl's vocation; Murphy, contradicting Frederick B. Adams, believes the fragment was intended for the end of the novel's penultimate book 6. At the least, the fragment raises interesting questions about Cather's changing intentions as she wrote. Certainly,
in this fragment *not* used, Willa Cather planned to keep her novel
focused on Cécile's future. The point for this study, however, is
that Cather ends her novel with a different focus and an arrestingly different epilogue that occurs fifteen years later. In this ending, the emphasis is on male errors of judgment.

The published fictional epilogue suggests that while the males in the novel live with their attention still fixed on the past, main facts about their present escape them. Cather based her novel on Parkman's five-volume *France and England in North America* (see Skaggs, "Cather's Use"). After the third volume on Frontenac (a central presence in Cather's novel), the fourth volume is titled *A Half-Century of Conflict*. This incessant conflict is, by implication, looming immediately ahead as Cather's novel begins in 1697. From the first line of this novel, Time—indicated by century, epoch, year, season, month, day, and hour—is running out. The novel proper begins as the last ship leaves the colony that will now be stranded during the long winter just ahead. According to Parkman, civic disorder begins in the next year, just as Frontenac dies and the Auclairs elect to stay in Canada.

Everything traced in the novel has changed by the time of the epilogue, but the men don't acknowledge it. Cécile's father, though "shocked at the change" in the figure of the returning Monseigneur (SR 270), accepts the statement that he himself "had scarcely changed at all" (272). He accepts the description of Quebec as a place "where nothing changes" (277), although all ascertainable historical facts, especially in Parkman, stress the opposite. When Euclide Auclair, the clear measurer, agrees that Quebec is changeless, he thus ignores his daughter. Cécile must certainly have changed, for she is now prospering as the affluent wife of Pierre Charron, formerly of Montreal, and has "four little boys" who are "the Canadians of the future" (278). This stable Charron family further suggests that their dominant father has changed, too; we are allowed to assume that he now stays closer to home, no longer identifying himself with perilous adventure in the surrounding wilderness.

The four sons added to Auclair's daughter also imply that Cather, in her last manuscript decision, accepted the change Faulkner had made in his newly configured Bundren "family of man" of 1930—four sons and a daughter. She will stick with that four-sons-and-a-daughter family as the "realest" fiction in her most "autobiographical" stories to come: "Old Mrs. Harris" and "The Best Years." The new configuration is a way these two writers salute each other and also acknowledge fictional emendations and distortions.

It might be worth mentioning, however, that the "rootedness," so distinctive to Anton Rosicky and Anse Bundren, is stressed in Cather's *discarded* ending to explain home-loving Cécile:

> [Staying put in Quebec], that was life, that was reality and security. Anything else was merely separation from one's good.
> People who have not been . . . held fast by their love of one spot on the rolling earth know nothing about it — cannot imagine it. It is a loyalty that has the force and blindness of a passion. Perhaps it is some biological survival, a feeling left over from some very remote past. (ccc)

When Cather *excises* these lines about Cécile, she relegates such "rootedness" to males. Immobility, changelessness, is not granted a mother of four little sons. Old Mrs. Harris herself feels "tied to the chariot of young life, [where she] had to go where it went" (omh 97). Even wheelchair-bound Sapphira, in Cather's last novel, most regrets being unable to ride horseback and thus cut a fine moving figure. In the intervening novel *Lucy Gayheart* (1935), the heroine is always remembered in motion. It's as if Cather catches herself, as Whitman says, on the verge of a usual mistake. She corrects it. Hereafter, in her last five books of fiction, she associates rootedness with males, not females. The idea traces back to Anton Rosicky and Anse Bundren, his dark shadow.

Having finished *Shadows on the Rock* in 1931, Cather turned her attention so immediately and intensely to "Old Mrs. Harris" that she did not even try to attend her mother's funeral in California. I have presented elsewhere several ways of looking at this brilliant story (Skaggs, "Teaching"). At this point I'm observing, however, that when Cather placed "Old Mrs. Harris" at the center of *Obscure Destinies*, before she could even get the story serialized, she was also pursuing another agenda. The completed volume shoved toward one sensitive reader a caustic corrective for his male portraits, his female portraits, his inherited stories, and his personal attitudes. In this light "Old Mrs. Harris" seems as patronizing a dismissal of *As I Lay Dying* as that novel seemed of "Neighbour Rosicky." By leading off with Rosicky and closing with "Two Friends," Cather made all three into an exploding package for the mailbox at Rowan Oak. Later, she even broke her own firm rule against allowing any of her work to be included in the anthologies of others. She permitted Rosicky alone to be anthologized in 1942.[2] In the anthology, Whit Burnett's *This Is My Best*, she insistently stood by her fictional man, whatever she imagined Faulkner had implied about him.

To review the grievances Cather might have felt after assimilating *As I Lay Dying*, one checks its title, its parental characters, its name puns, and its glaring eyes. Cather, after all, has gone to school with Emerson and Poe, both of whom pun on the eye-I-aye homophones. At the least, Faulkner subtracts the "ayes" from his eye-similes and transparent eyeballs. Beyond these annoyances, however, Faulkner seemed to bury in *As I Lay Dying* a putdown of every novel Cather had written. For example, as in *Alexander's Bridge*, here too a bridge sags, sways, and drops men in a river; but nobody in Faulkner's river drowns, denigrating the crisis. When she herself had reversed this item, as was her habit, Cather mentioned a sagging bridge over the Sweetwater, also safely traversed by foot in *A Lost Lady*. But Cather's bridge furnishes only anxiety and pathos; in *As I Lay Dying* it supplies harsh comedy and pain. In Cather's *O Pioneers!* a hostile terrain menaces those who try to farm it, before it finally submits to the plow; Faulkner's Mississippi denies farmer Bundren any of Alexandra's eventual economic prosperity, because he himself does not work in his fields or make plans for enhancing the future: his farming won't pay. Charles A. Peek's emphasis that the Bundrens' "failure to either alter or escape their world is an indictment of many of our cherished myths" (Hamblin and Peek 23) seems especially relevant here.

As in Cather's *Song of the Lark*, a protagonist in Faulkner can "lift a weight greater than himself," for ironically, Jewel repeatedly saves Addie's heavy coffin, though he provokes awe without concomitant approval or praise. As in *My Ántonia*, a daughter falls into an illicit pregnancy, but reacts evasively by seeking an abortion rather than treasuring her child. As in *One of Ours*, we glimpse a bleakly negative farm life, but gain no redeeming camaraderie of war for the pleasurable relief of those who can escape to fight (as Darl has). As in *A Lost Lady* (not to mention *The Sound and the Fury*), Faulkner emphasizes a lost woman, without any of the gaiety associated with "that long lost lady laugh." As in *The Professor's House*, the conveyance transporting Faulkner's Mother Eve—or Mother Addie, whose father said she was born to stay dead a long time—carries her off-balance before leaving her at the bottom of a dark drop. As in *My Mortal Enemy*, the most powerful female figure lies dying, but Myra dies in the last half of the novel, while Addie lies dying in the first half and does not live to see the dawn. As in *Death Comes for the Archbishop*, we seek what it means "to die"—*ad die*—while the "vaillantly" optimistic Cora Tull seems blasphemous in her insistent piety.

Further, *As I Lay Dying* seems to corrupt Cather's best work by making the simultaneously linear and cyclical structure of *My Ántonia* a comedy or parody, while turning its "burdens" into Bundrens, and making the very "family of man" central symbol as off-balance as Addie's coffin: the controlling mother dies instead of the weak father, and the children are four controlled males and only one anarchic female. To "answer" this Anse-Bundren-created distortion, Cather *retained* that family pattern and claimed it intimately for her own, through the microcosmic Templetons of "Old Mrs. Harris," as well as the Ferguessons—strident eye-sign-named family, of "The Best Years," her other late-career "autobiographical" short story. In this last story Cather wrote, she in turn included an equivalent review or positive nod to every novel she had written — *as well as to the three stories* of *Obscure Destinies* (see Skaggs, "Icons and Willa Cather"). In both the late and the unmistakably autobiographical Cather stories we find a strong mother, weak father, single daughter, and four sons — the family pattern of *As I Lay Dying*. And then hers. Donald Kartiganer remarks on "the cunning of Anse" that enables him "to replace the shock of death with what is . . . self-interest or the mind-consuming practice of craft" (*Fragile Thread* 26). Though Mrs. Harris is equally surrounded in her lifetime by her self-absorbed family, they register her death acutely, to judge by the story's stunning last sentence.

Old Mrs. Harris, "hárassed" in daily life as severely as Addie was, is the focal figure of this brilliant story, which is complex enough to compete with *As I Lay Dying*. Cather's tour de force story is also her first to stress her own *concision* as a competitive advantage (Faulkner will show her what he thinks of it in *Absalom, Absalom!* — which began as a story [Williamson 243]). I will deal here only with the elements of "Old Mrs. Harris" that make a comment on Faulkner's preceding novel. That doesn't shorten the task at hand, however, because *every* detail eventually seems relevant, as every part of "Neighbour Rosicky" seems addressed within Faulkner's novel, including the characters of Rosicky's family members. We start by observing that Faulkner changed the essentially positive portraits of the *Ántonia* family to negative ones: Ántonia/Mary becomes Addie, Cuzak/Rosicky becomes Anse, that Burden whom Ántonia loves like her own becomes the several Bundrens.

Then "Old Mrs. Harris" changes their characters back again. In the process, "the family" is bitterly criticized: "What were families for, anyway!" adolescent Vickie spits, when she feels abandoned (OMH 186); her mother Victoria feels just as negatively "that the house and the people in it were choking her to death" (175). But Grandma Harris knows she and her grandsons "had in common the realest and truest things" (184) and that "the moment she heard the children running down the uncarpeted back stairs, she forgot to be low. Indeed, she ceased to be an individual, an old woman with aching feet; she became part of a group, became a relationship" (136–37). Families *are* the realest and truest things in *this* Cather fiction, as contrasted to Cather's bitter *One of Ours*, where this two-writer bittersweet literary relationship started.

All characters in Cather's story experience death. "Mrs. Harris knew she was failing" (170), but keeps on going "when each step cost her something" (as it will cost Cash something for the rest of his life). She is not alone, however, for everybody in the household grieves for the cat Blue Boy, before grieving for Grandma. Yet all contribute willingly to the living and grieving group, and serve it, as they also *receive* from it what they *value* most. All have their assigned chores and often enjoy performing them. Even the baby Hughie smiles to charm their critical neighbor Mrs. Rosen. And critical or not, the Rosens support the Templetons *because they admire or envy them*, not out of hypocritical duty, as Cora Tull understands it in Faulkner's novel. That neighborly relation is the first thing Cather takes up in her first sentence. Later, waspish church ladies at the Methodist lawn party snipe at Victoria, as church men snipe at Anse, but Victoria proudly surmounts their criticism, with the supportive approval of her children. The difference in these Cather and Faulkner family groups is not their poverty, their hard work, or their deep grief, but their genuine, family-wide, if occasional, satisfactions.

Of particular interest is the way in which Cather changes Addie's characterization through the mother Victoria Templeton. For more than one reader, the most startlingly negative fact about Faulkner's Addie is her admission, when she is allowed to speak for herself, that she enjoyed beating her school pupils: "I would look forward to the times when they faulted, so I could whip them," she says (170); at the end of the school day, "I could be quiet and hate them" (169). In this glimpse of Addie's character, Faulkner in fact picks up a motif from *The Song of the Lark*. Just before sailing for Europe, fledgling soprano Thea Kronborg has experienced "troubled sleep" during which "that night she taught in Moonstone again: she beat her pupils in hideous rages, she kept on beating them" (Penguin ed., 317). When dead Addie speaks of her children, she says, "My children were of me alone, of the wild blood boiling along the earth, of me and of all that lived, of none and of all" (175). Cather's mother-figure, like Addie, also picks up a whip in "Old Mrs. Harris," as Victoria orders her sons into her room, "where she heard explanations and administered punishment." Cather adds, "When she whipped them, she did it thoroughly" (145–46). The point made, however, is that she also gives them love, and they love her in return, in spite of her punishments. Cather changes the *tone* of these described whippings, not the acts; she denies that the act, itself, is reprehensible. But Victoria uses common sense in her disciplining. Learning the reason her sons left the home before breakfast without informing her, she desists in the disciplining; for their grandmother has ordered them to bury Blue Boy decently, and that has seemed to them the greater obligation. Faulkner's Darl guesses correctly that Addie has beat Jewel hardest because she loves him best; Cather's Victoria is impartial and just. But both mothers whip or beat children.

Both mothers are also arrestingly "self-absorbed," even legalistic in their views of childbearing and how much of it they should be required to do. Victoria "was sick of it all; sick of dragging this chain of life that never let her rest and periodically knotted and overpowered her; made her ill and hideous for months, and then dropped another baby into her arms" (178). Addie calculates how many babies she owes Anse to compensate for the "time out" that produced Jewel; but neither mother loves childbearing. Yet the most remarkable part of this contrasting portrayal of mothers may be Mr. Rosen's suggestion, in "Old Mrs. Harris," that selfish mothers may be best because they can rear unselfish children, as the Templeton family proves. For that matter, Addie's children also prove surprisingly unselfish from time to time. Not even selfish mothers coupled with weak fathers inevitably make a family dysfunctional. Dysfunction is in the eye of the beholder. Most of Faulkner's beholders, smelling Addie's corpse, see trouble.

Small details in "Old Mrs. Harris" keep correcting *As I Lay Dying*. Cora's bad cakes transform into Grandma Harris's splendid white cake with coconut icing—the one the neighbors want at the ice cream social. Cora's acidic judgments reappear as Mrs. Jackson's viperish insinuations, which Victoria hates but gets over. The evangelical hypocrisies of Whitfield and his congregants become the inclusive Methodist town social which can stretch even to include "dreary little Maudes," each of whom has a different father. Dessert-loving Victoria makes sure the Maudes get their share of sweets.

The road that seems so threatening to a man, as Anse defines it, is both served and controlled by Cather's Roadmaster, who helps Vickie leave, compete for a scholarship, and return home again. The Rosens, in fact, stroll along that road out of town, because it "led toward the moon" (121). Addie's burning eyes that seem like two candles (*AILD* 8) reappear in the "old lion's head" of Grandma Harris and remind us that cat's or tiger's eyes burn bright in the forests of the night, even though Blue Boy, the family tomcat that goes "skylarking" in summer (as Darl and Cash suspect Jewel of doing), dies of distemper—as also does, in effect, Old Mrs. Harris. Addie's bedroom, which Cora makes so unappealing with its little-ironed sheets and shuck mattress (8), becomes Old Mrs. Harris's "hideous cluttered room" (80) with a "narrow spindle-framed lounge" (78) and "thin mattress" with no springs (80), the setting in which children hear their favorite books. Correspondences multiply.

Two main things in "Old Mrs. Harris," however, might have

offended William Faulkner: Cather's implication that he knows nothing about women, and her insinuation that he misrepresents southernness. Cather, of course, was also a Virginian and a southerner until her ninth year. Her resort to ostensibly "autobiographical" experience in this story (which is a device she uses, I believe, when she is nervous or anxious about the success of something difficult that she's trying to accomplish)[3] establishes her southern credentials and thereby carries a contest to Faulkner's little postage stamp of native soil. It doesn't seem a friendly way to talk, as the neighbors say in *Sapphira*, another "autobiographical" fiction, but it's still the voice we can hear.

Consider that title "Three Women," which Cather initially planned to use instead of "Old Mrs. Harris." It is actually referred to in the dust-jacket flap copy for the *April Twilights* edition of 1938. All the three women living in the Templeton family seem outside or beyond Faulkner's vision, insofar as he has expressed it by this 1932 publication point. Vickie is a young person who wants an education for her romance, not a man. Victoria is a strong, selfish, self-indulgent, handsome, admirable mother, whose children rise up and call her blessed. And Grandma Harris works for the family because doing so empowers her and makes her feel useful: fulfilled. Mrs. Rosen, the representative spokesperson of a critical Judeo-Christian point of view, admires them all, if sometimes grudgingly.[4] Vickie feels the world is against her when she's thwarted and turns her face to the wall; that's an adolescent despair for you, Cather shrugs. But Vickie also wins her scholarship and gets herself to college by using her head, because she "just wants" her education. The Rosens assure her that she'll not be disappointed if she starts with such pure desire, and that she'll "*be* something" (158, 156): community-approved future accomplishment is a new promise for a fictional lass. Her mother Victoria, conversely, is the nation's first sexually active and magnetic fictional mother who is also considered a success, who has the admiration of the town's businessmen, the courtly love of her husband, the indulgence of her long-suffering mother, and the pride of her children. Admittedly, she also "wanted to run away, back to Tennessee, and lead a free, gay life, as she had *when she first married*" (178, italics mine). But being young and married is not so bad, either. And Mrs. Harris, distinctly different from either her daughter or her granddaughter, "could have no real unhappiness while the children were well, and good, and fond of her and their mother" (136).

Grandma Harris is not without negative opinions: "The fault Grandmother found in Vickie was that she wasn't foolish enough. When the foolish girl married and began to have children, everything must give way to that. She must be humoured and given the best of everything, because having children was hard on a woman, and it was the most important thing in the world. . . . That was the great difference: in Tennessee there had been plenty of helpers" (180). Yet Grandma Harris, by choice, is "tied to the chariot of young life" (97). She acknowledges that "everything that's alive has got to suffer" (141). But she is neither a victim nor a martyr, nor even particularly dissatisfied, though intermittently annoyed. These three women, in short, as well as their neighbor Mrs. Rosen, are as complex as Cleopatra, whatever roles they fill. They know many sides to many questions, and bring many skills to bear on their quandaries and riddles, whether they are "educated" or not. They certainly do not merely mate, "litter," and die, as Doc Peabody states poor women do in *As I Lay Dying*. All of them find their own lives interesting, with or without children.

It is, however, on the matter of how much he really knows about his native land that Cather seems deliberately to spear Faulkner's liver. Her Templetons, after all, are from nearby Tennessee. First of all, she reminds him that in these back-home towns, dialects are spoken by the high as well as the low, Compsons as well as Gibsons. Mrs. Rosen, recognized for her "superior cultivation which made everything she did an exercise of skill" (135), has the most distinctive accent in Cather's story—a German lisp. But Grandma Harris with her old lion's head (suggesting The Goddess) also speaks ungrammatically, as "lower class" persons would, while remaining the person of most compelling interest to Mrs. Rosen, a class boundary crosser. The "bound servant" Mandy speaks like Grandma, only more so (138), while she also resides in a "snappy little Western democracy" (133) — a phrase that denies her class category as the town disapproves of her servant status. Grandma asks indignantly, "Air you two boys going to let that Mexican take Blue Boy and throw him on to some trash-pile? . . . You git up early in the morning, and I'll put him in a sack, and one of you take a spade and go to that crooked old willer tree . . . and dig a little grave . . . and bury him right" (144–45). The *dialects* raise doubts about Faulkner's rendering of hierarchical class structures. The Templetons are both elitist enough to be saluted and trashy enough to embarrass their neighbor; they are southern aristocrats and white trash simultaneously. Their *bound-servant,* who lives with them in snappy, democratic Colorado, raises questions about the exclusivity of the "peculiar institution." Mandy the servant girl, in fact, is Caucasian, not black. All Cather's characters refuse to stay in stereotypic postures and patterns.

When the story describes life "back home" in Tennessee, it does so thoroughly. The passage begins in Mrs. Harris's perplexity because neighbors criticize their household arrangements:

She didn't know why the neighbours acted so. . . . At home, back in Tennessee, her place in the family was not exceptional, but perfectly regular. Mrs. Harris had replied to Mrs. Rosen, when that lady asked why in the world she didn't break Vickie in to help her in the kitchen: "We are only young once, and trouble comes soon enough." Young girls, in the South, were supposed to be carefree and foolish. . . . In Tennessee every young married woman in good circumstances had an older woman in the house, a mother or mother-in-law or an old aunt, who managed the household economies and directed the help.

... To be sure, Mrs. Harris, and the other women of her age who managed their daughter's house, kept in the background; but it was their own background, and they ruled it jealously. They left the front porch and parlour to the young married couple and their young friends; the old women spent most of their lives in the kitchen and pantries and back dining-room. But there they ordered life to their own taste, entertained their friends, dispensed charity, and heard the troubles of the poor. Moreover, back there it was Grandmother's own house they lived in.

... The Templeton's troubles began when Mr. Templeton's aunt died and left him a few thousand dollars, and he got the idea of bettering himself.... Here, in Skyline, ... Mrs. Harris was no longer living in a feudal society, where there were plenty of landless people glad to render service to the more fortunate. (130–33)

If the society "back home" is feudal, they like it that way.

Finally, then, "Old Mrs. Harris" and "Two Friends" would have been as offensive to William Faulkner as *As I Lay Dying* had apparently been to Willa Cather. He was not one to suffer insults generously, but he may have responded prophetically, before he knew he was hit. Though *Absalom, Absalom!* would be his brilliant and most effective answer, it would take many years to finish. *Light in August*, well under way and constantly in Faulkner's thoughts and conversation, followed almost immediately. But *before* he could have held *Obscure Destinies* in hand, we read that Faulkner and Cather were together in the same space at the same time. In 1931, as Blotner tells the story, after *Sanctuary* (published in February of 1931) had caused such scandal, and after *Shadows on the Rock* (published in August of 1931) had become such a best-seller, Faulkner and Dashiell Hammett were lunching with

Bennett Cerf when they heard that Cerf was invited to a black-tie dinner that evening at the Knopf home, along with Willa Cather. The two persuaded Cerf to secure them invitations, then drank through the afternoon and did not change clothes. Cerf no doubt picked them up at dinnertime with severe qualms; but they both insisted on going. Hammett quietly passed out before dinner was served, and Faulkner collapsed as he made his exit. No conversation between Faulkner and Cather is recorded (Blotner 1:742; Blotner 293–94). But the evening must have left an impression on all of them.

By November 1931 Faulkner had been identified in print as "America's most promising author" (Blotner 288). He was on his way to Hollywood, to make money as a successful and powerful man should. He later told Ben Wasson, relative to his views on women at this time, "You know what I was saying when I wrote *Sanctuary* don't you? I was saying that women are impervious to evil" (Blotner 294). Some might argue that Cather's continuing interest in his work after this dinner-party performance proved his point.

Upon turning to *Light in August*, we must first and last take account of the links that bind it to *My Ántonia*. Lena Grove, spiritual daughter of Lena Lingard (see Gardam) who initiated Jim Burden sexually, walks in that present tense Cather first experimented with in *O Pioneers!* toward an anticipated rendezvous with her lover, Lucas Burch, in turn modeled after Ántonia's betrayer, the feckless flirt Larry Donovan. In the town of Jefferson, named as obviously for a nature-loving leader as was the town of Black Hawk, Lena meets instead the inauspicious Byron Bunch, who needs her attention even more than Jim Burden needed Lena Lingard's. Both Lenas have acquired good town manners quickly, as a matter of self-preservation. Lena Grove has learned, as did Lena Lingard, to tell or shape her own story her way, that is, to take charge of her own meaning, before the "women who are good without being kind" (*LA* 6) can do it for her. Those women

do it for Lena Lingard and the Widow Steavens does it for Ántonia. At the end, both Lenas are still curious to see how far they
can travel before they stop; Lena Lingard has gotten to where the
land runs out in San Francisco; Lena Grove is already in Tennessee ("Old Mrs. Harris" country, when she might as well have
gotten to Louisiana instead, by assuming that young man Burch
would go west). Both Lenas enjoy masculine company as they
move around, and neither is in any hurry to marry. Lena Lingard
explains, "But, you know, my weakness is playthings" (240).

The Burdens of both places are strangers in town and should
just be passing through, as the song goes. Jim Burden of Black
Hawk is a southerner, and the Burdens of Jefferson are Yankees.
Yet the Jefferson Burdens lack descendants as much as childless
Jim Burden does, for their last representative lies decapitated
outside her burning house as Lena reaches town. In Faulkner's
novel the main characters — Lena Grove, Reverend Hightower,
Joe Christmas, Byron Bunch, Joanna Burden — are all orphans,
as Jim Burden is, a quintupling of the orphan's dilemma, as *The
Sound and the Fury* doubled the two beginnings of *My Ántonia*
and *As I Lay Dying* multiplied its different points of view.

Joe Christmas, to my surprise, is also linked to *My Ántonia*.
He serves to answer the challenge of how to outdo Wick Cutter, the usurous rapist, murderer, and suicide, whom Jim Burden
said was "different from any other rascal I have ever known" (*MA*
213) — that is, who is unique. Assuming that Faulkner must have
been aware of how obsessively he had been recalling *My Ántonia*,
one can imagine several rhetorical questions he asked and answered here. For example, what is worse than Wick Cutter? One
answer is a black rapist murderer who's not positive he's black.
What is worse than throwing a bride to the wolves? Raping, de-
bauching, and deserting a mate. What's the most awful form of
suicide a man can arrange? Provoking castration before death.
What provokes these dreadful questions? Believing with memory before knowing remembers a child's terrible helplessness, the

kind Joe Christmas has assimilated until the moment he became a man. The questions ought to have started by now, as Faulkner would say when he needed an explanatory device. But even Joe Christmas's name—which "can be somehow an augur of what he will do, if other men can only read the meaning in time" (*LA* 29)—has antecedent augurs in Joe's fellow wanderers from *My Ántonia*, Jake Marpole and Otto Fuchs of reverberant names.

In *My Ántonia*, the hired girls, who work or congregate at the Boys Home Hotel, hear Blind d'Arnault play "My Old Kentucky Home" while the guests "sang one Negro melody after another" (*MA* 105). *Light in August* begins by echoing such a Stephen Foster song, Cather style. Lena Grove muses, "I have come from Alabama," and a reader hums, "With a banjo on my knee." Continuing the song, "And I'm goin' to Louisiana," we nod as Lena also continues, "Although I have not been quite a month on the road I am already in Mississippi." She adds, "Further from home than I have ever been before," and we hear a jaunty refrain, "Oh, Susanna, oh don't you cry for me, for I'm going to Louisiana with my baby on my knee." Instead, of course, she eventually penetrates Tennessee.

Hightower traces back to *The Professor's House*. In Tom Outland's story the center of Cliff City is a noteworthy tower, "the fine thing that held all the jumble of houses together and made them mean something" (*PH* 201). That tower gives the ruin meaning, as ruined Hightower, serving as its "moral center," makes Faulkner's novel mean something. Even at his worst, "there remains yet something of honor and pride, of life" about him (*LA* 53). He is especially tied thematically to Joanna Burden, since both had a grandfather who was shot down in the streets of Jefferson, and both have lived lives shaped by that event: one dies and one is born to new life.

Finally, however, it is Joanna (the Joan-na/Jonah who is swallowed up by a whale of a story), the desecrated caricature bearing the Cather-associated name *Burden*, who mandates our attention.

First, she has "a face quiet, grave, utterly unalarmed" and "a voice calm, a little deep, quite cold" (*LA* 218). Then "she told him she *was forty.* 'Which means fortyone or fortynine* from the way she said it,' he thought" (219, my italics; Cather reduced her age by three years, but was forty-seven in 1921, when she and Faulkner probably met). Cather surrogate Joanna Burden accepts her male lover, Joe Christmas, with "hard, untearful and unselfpitying and almost manlike yielding . . . [and] surrender," while she "shows the strength and fortitude of a man" (221).

Soon Joanna is "living not alone in sin but in filth. She had an avidity for the forbidden wordsymbols. . . . She revealed the terrible and impersonal curiosity of a child about forbidden subjects and objects; that rapt and tireless and detached interest of a surgeon in the physical body and its possibilities" (244). Speaking for Christmas, Faulkner adds, "Soon she more than shocked him: she astonished and bewildered him" (244). She can fly into jealous rages, for "it was as if she had invented the whole thing deliberately, for the purpose of playing it out like a play. [One recalls Cécile of *Shadows on the Rock* saying, "Oh, everything we do, my father and I is a kind of play" (*SR* 58).] Yet she did it with such fury . . . he thought that she was mad" (*LA* 245).

Joe Christmas believes Joanna "spent a certain portion of each day sitting tranquilly at a desk writing tranquilly" (224), but finds "she revealed an unexpected and infallible instinct for intrigue" (*LA* 245). Indeed, "he would find her naked . . . in the wild throes of nymphomania" (245); "she began to corrupt him. He began to be afraid" (246). Yet "the affair went on, submerging him more and more by the imperious and overriding fury of those nights. Perhaps he realized that he could not escape" (246). So Christmas utters the most cutting words he can summon: "You're old. I never noticed that before. An old woman. . . . You're not any good any more" (262). When he realizes that she intends either to kill him or force him into her mode, he slits her throat.

When their stories got too harrowing, these two master tale

spinners both learned they did *not* have to settle for just one ending. Epilogues add two to *Shadows on the Rock* and *Sapphira and the Slave Girl*. *Death Comes for the Archbishop* has two or three endings (the mutual blessing; Vaillant's death; Latour's death) as *The Sound and the Fury* has four, or five if we count the appendix. The mentor of both, Mark Twain, constructs seven for *A Connecticut Yankee in King Arthur's Court*. This chapter uses only a couple.

Presciently, Joe Christmas realizes before he strikes Joanna down that "it was as though some enemy upon whom he had wreaked his utmost of violence and contumely stood, unscathed and unscarred, and contemplated him with a musing and insufferable contempt" (224). In such a scene Faulkner traces boomeranging suspicion, projection, defensive assault. The woman's impervious and will-full contempt seems to merit male violence.

Faulkner himself repelled suspected contempt, according to Blotner, with verbal assaults. For example, while Faulkner was in Hollywood, having put *Light in August* aside uncompleted, he enjoyed hunting with Howard Hawks.

One of the director's friends, Clark Gable, had a .410 over-and-under shotgun that Faulkner admired so much he wanted one like it. The first time they had driven into the Imperial Valley for some dove-hunting, Hawks began to talk about books. He would remember the conversation clearly. Faulkner entered it, but Gable remained silent. Finally he ventured a question.

"Mr. Faulkner," he said, "what do you think somebody should read if he wants to read the best modern books? Who would you say are the best living writers?"

After a moment Faulkner answered. "Ernest Hemingway, Willa Cather, Thomas Mann, John Dos Passos, and myself."

Gable took a moment to absorb the information. "Oh," he said. "Do you write?"

"Yes, Mr. Gable," Faulkner replied. "What do you do?" (Blotner 310)

7

Tit for Tat

LIGHT IN AUGUST seemed to leave even William Faulkner feeling ambivalent. He stated, "I seemed to have a vision of it and the other ones subsequent to *The Sound and the Fury* ranked in order upon a shelf while I looked at the titled backs . . . with a flagging attention which was almost distaste" (Blotner 311). Willa Cather, on the other hand, took a deep breath and constructed a reply, delivered, it would seem, under an arched eyebrow. It arrives in an essay entitled "148 Charles Street," after which dull title the merely curious browsers could be trusted to pass on. The book in which this essay serves as centerpiece is entitled *Not Under Forty*. The book title, of course, could be read one way by the creator of that fictional Joanna Burden, who lied that her age was merely forty, while it would send other readers on a detour. But William Faulkner, who was thirty-nine when *Not Under Forty* was published, had at least the warning DO NOT ENTER HERE to compel him to open the volume. He would find a *series* of comments to ponder hard.

Cather supplied her first-time or literal-minded reader with these intriguing words pointing a detour arrow in the form of a prefatory note:

The title of this book is meant to be "arresting" only in the literal sense, like the signs put up for motorists: "ROAD UNDER REPAIR," etc. It means that the book will have little interest for people under forty years of age. The world broke in two in 1922 or thereabouts, and the persons and prejudices recalled in these sketches slid back into yesterday's seven thousand years. Thomas Mann, to be sure, belongs immensely to the forward-goers, and they are concerned only with his forwardness. But he also goes back a long way, and his backwardness is more gratifying to the backward. It is for the backward, and by one of their number, that these sketches were written.

One reader might recall that in the last glimpse of Catheresque Joanna Burden she was backward-looking because her decapitated head was face-backward.

For the many general readers of *Not Under Forty*, the prefatory note raised speculation in every line, and still does. As a matter of "design" in this collection of essays with its own integrity, the flagged date 1922 ends the volume as well as beginning it. It's also just in the middle, for not only was it the year when the world broke in two, announced in the prefatory note; it was also the year when young genius Katherine Mansfield, hailed in the last essay, stopped writing in her journal "some months before her [untimely] death" (*NUF* 138). The volume suggests that for Katherine Mansfield, the world broke in two because approaching death killed her impulse to record herself spontaneously. I have argued elsewhere[1] that Cather was referencing in this line about world breakage Henry James's novel *Roderick Hudson*, in which the statement is made that no genius is permitted to create works out of youthful energy and verve more than six times. After that, any important creation must emerge from discipline and technique. After Cather had collapsed her two volumes of short stories into one, her sixth fiction was *One of Ours*, published in 1922. The world broke in two because her work hereafter, she felt in retrospect, would be difficult and demanding, and not at all "a child's attitude toward everything [which] is an artist's attitude" (*Lark* 460 [1st ed.]). That child's attitude is what Thea is still relying on at the end of *The Song of the Lark*, but as the novel ends she's still *under* forty (465). Faulkner's sixth novel, coincidentally, is *Sanctuary*. *Light in August* would have been the first to need, by the standards of early James, harder work and seasoned discipline, not merely youthful energy.

The year 1922 is also when *One of Ours* was published, including its admiring portrait of Faulkner-lookalike Victor Morse. It's the year that could be said to start the real relationship between Cather and Faulkner. To salute its publication year at the beginning of this collection of essays is to salute the relationship itself as a BCE/AD divide affecting the perception of time and history. That's a remarkable tribute to William Faulkner. No wonder he saluted her in return!

One asks, when attention is arrested by that prefatory note in *Not Under Forty*, exactly what roads need repairing here? What avenues of communication are torn up? What matters of taste need reviewing on that road under repair? When we recall that Thomas Mann, plus Cather, appeared on Faulkner's list of the five greatest modern writers mentioned at the end of the last chapter, and that Mann also appears in an appreciative tribute in *Not Under Forty*, then we recognize that both of our sparring pair salute Mann's greatness. Cather here applauds the traditional, biblically rooted *Joseph and His Brothers* as the Mann she especially values. Her essay on Mann, in fact, may provide the keynote theme for Faulkner's Nobel Prize speech. In Cather's highlighting Mann's claims to write of "the nature of man," Cather herself defines that nature as "a double nature, struggling with itself" (*NUF* 96). That is not far from "the human heart in conflict with itself," which alone makes good writing (Mintner 218). In any case, we now register that the Faulkner novel that followed *Not Under Forty* of 1936 was Bible-referencing *Absalom, Absalom!* of 1938, which also boasts an exclamation point like *O Pioneers! Absalom, Ab-*

salom! suggests as much backward looking as any one of that group could wish for. The volume did not go unremarked by Willa Cather.

In *Not Under Forty*, Cather's most direct comments on William Faulkner are imbedded in her riveting essay on Annie Fields that precedes "Miss Jewett." Sarah Orne Jewett is a subject that draws off the attention of literary people who know nothing of 148 Charles Street, and perhaps never notice that Faulkner is named there, after a putdown of D. H. Lawrence. In this naming, Cather breaks all her own rules about publicly discussing currently living authors. When she actually drops these two names into her text, she excuses herself by quoting the sentence of an eponymous schoolboy. But for Faulkner, at least, the sentence still conveys her admiration, ambivalence, and naughty wit, as well as the attention he deserves: "D. H. Lawrence is rather rated a back number here, but Faulkner keeps his end up" (*NUF* 74)

How she gets to that sentence, of course, is interesting. We can't trace it, because she burned all her letters. Here she emphasizes that she is writing an addendum to a previously published appreciation of Mrs. Fields; the explanation allows her to stress the current date as she writes: *1936*. The date, in turn, clearly follows the publication of *Light in August* in 1932. She has had four years to think about it. And whatever she may have said about her age when she was younger, nearer Joanna Burden's age, she's now over sixty and wiser, as well as more mature, unlike some younger folk she could mention who needn't bother to listen to her, not at all.

"148 Charles Street" displays as uninviting a title as can be. The third of six pieces, this essay also begins and ends in the present, as does *Light in August*. In further mentioning Mrs. Fields's admiration for Shakespeare's *Henry IV*, she also picks up the fact, remembered by at least one, that Hightower turns to *Henry IV* at the end of *Light in August* in order to find "food for a man" when he feels as if he no longer needs Tennyson. Mrs. Fields also admires and reads *Henry IV*, however, so the play must also be food for a woman, a point to recall when we return to this play in "Before Breakfast." *Henry IV* will be the drama over which these two producers face off, at the end of their lives. Their confrontation is a bit like Bolingbroke and Mowbray in *Richard II*, which precedes *Henry IV* and is also relevant to both of them. Cather especially allows her essay on Mrs. Fields to stress twilight, Faulkner's and Hightower's favorite time, when Hightower hears the galloping hooves of the past. This is Cather's version of twilight in "148 Charles Street":

> It was at tea-time, I used to think, that the great shades were most likely to appear; sometimes they seemed to come up the deeply carpeted stairs, along with living friends. At that hour the long room was dimly lighted, the fire bright, and through the wide windows the sunset was flaming, or softly brooding, upon the Charles River and the Cambridge shore beyond. The ugliness of the world, all possibility of wrenches and jars and wounding contacts, seemed securely shut out. It was indeed the peace of the past, where the tawdry and cheap have been eliminated and the enduring things have taken their proper, happy places. (62–63)

The parallels between this passage and our last views of Hightower are striking. However, this passage was previously printed in 1922 in a review of sorts called "The House on Charles Street,"[2] the "house" of which creates a more appealing title. The essay's prior appearance again brings up questions about who described twilight first, and for what audience. But, of course, even to ask the question one must assume Faulkner saw the newspaper publication, a chancy matter. In any case, Willa Cather remembered the piece and suddenly hauled it out again and put it in the center of her only collection of essays (until another appeared posthumously). Whatever the triggering circumstance, the reference to *Henry IV* follows the twilight scene immediately, in both versions. Cather always stressed *juxtaposition*.[3]

The remarkable "148 Charles Street" starts twice and ends twice, as both our writers have been doing for some time now. In its genesis it was an "appreciation" of a book by M. A. DeWolfe Howe called *Memories of a Hostess*, about Mrs. Fields and by her literary executor. More important, the warm memories of Annie Fields that Willa Cather expressed here are arrestingly similar, in numerous details, to parts of *A Lost Lady*, which she was also writing in 1922. Does that mean Annie Fields is one prototype for Marian Forrester, or that good phrases and details recycle themselves in works written concomitantly? That fictional lost lady was certainly lodged in William Faulkner's brain as well: besides his "Une Ballade des Femmes Perdues," there are the two lost ladies of *The Sound and the Fury*, and those in his other works such as *Sanctuary*. It doesn't seem entirely haphazard that Willa Cather chose to remind at least *him* of what she'd said in 1922 about matters concerning them both. She has her unnamed schoolboy concede, of course, that he's done well in working up his version of the material.

Annie Fields gained access to the literary world through her January-May marriage, Forrester-like, to James T. Fields of Tichnor and Fields, Publishers. The firm "published everybody," and the house of its partner entertained "the aristocracy of letters and arts" (*nuf* 56) as Marian Forrester entertained the "railroad aristocracy" (*all* 9). All Cather readers recall Marian's charming laugh. Of Annie Fields's laugh, Cather explains:

> I had seldom heard so young, so merry, so musical a laugh; a laugh with countless shades of relish and appreciation and kindness in it. And, on occasion, a short laugh from that same fragile source could positively do police duty! It could put an end to a conversation that had taken an unfortunate turn,

absolutely dismiss and silence impertinence or presumption. No woman could have been so great a hostess, could have made so many highly developed personalities happy under her roof, could have blended so many strongly specialized and keenly sensitive people in her drawing-room, without having a great power to control and organize. It was a power so sufficient that one seldom felt it as one lived in the harmonious atmosphere it created—an atmosphere in which one seemed absolutely safe from everything ugly. (57–58)

William Faulkner will soon demonstrate in *Absalom, Absalom!* that nobody is absolutely safe from anything ugly, and Willa Cather will pay attention to what he says there. But even Marian Forrester knows, in *A Lost Lady*, that when common sense dictates otherwise, it can still be pleasant to say, "Oh, that, I'm afraid is a pretty dream. But we'll dream it, anyway!" (*ALL* 35). This fictional lost lady has inherited all "the magic of contradictions" (79), much like Annie Fields, who will never be entirely lost because of Willa Cather's expressed admiration. It is possible, too, to link the *negative* contradictions of this magnetic duo to the Old Beauty, Gabrielle Longstreet, in the posthumous volume that ends with Cather's last words to Faulkner.

The same language suggesting throughout Cather's work that life can be dramatic, as well as a drama, a play, or a theatrical performance, is noticeable as well in *A Lost Lady*,[4] and also attends her portrait of Annie Fields: "One rejoiced in her little triumphs over colour-destroying age and its infirmities, as at the play one rejoices in the escape of the beautiful and frail from the pursuit of things powerful and evil. It was a drama in which the heroine must be sacrificed in the end: but for how long did she make the outward voyage delightful, with how many a *divertissement* and bright scene did she illumine the respite and the long wait at Aulis!" (*NUF* 59). Niel Herbert says it with similar intensity at the end of *A Lost Lady*:

He came to be very glad that he had known her, and that she had had a hand in breaking him in to life. He has known pretty women and clever ones since then, — but never one like her, as she was in her best days. . . . He would like to call up the shade of the young Mrs. Forrester, as the witch of Endor called up Samuel's and challenge it, demand the secret of that ardour; ask her whether she had really found some ever-blooming, ever-burning, ever-piercing joy, or whether it was all fine play-acting. Probably she had found no more than another; but she had always the power of suggesting things much lovelier than herself, as the perfume of a single flower may call up the whole sweetness of spring. (ALL 171–72)

In their later years, both ladies — fictional Marian and factual Annie — "sit and look out over a shrinking kingdom" but never lose their capacity for gaiety (NUF 67). Both have "the very genius of survival" (67). In this unabashedly affirmative essay, we get to admire survival without experiencing any of the ethical questions it creates in the more complex novel. In fact, if Faulkner did happen to read this core piece when it appeared first in 1922, that unqualified admiration may have bothered him. Certainly in 1936, after *Not Under Forty* was published, Cather said in a letter to Thomas Masaryk that she was sending him a collection of essays, including "148 Charles Street," and then, in a Freudian slip, dates the letter December 1, 1923 (the year *A Lost Lady* was published), instead of 1936 (Stout, *Calendar*, no. 1334). She herself seems subliminally aware of the connection.

This essay seems designed not only to grab Faulkner's attention and prove that both writer and reader were playing like chess masters in a championship tournament, but also to teach him some lessons by using Annie Fields as a witch of Endor who could summon shades to speak the truth. The first lesson, in its third sentence, is that old things such as the old Parker House hotel in Boston are often nicer than "modernized" — or perhaps *modernist*—ones (*NUF* 52). The "very charming old lady" Cather sets out from the Parker House to meet, of course, can transmogrify to Rosa Coldfield of *Absalom, Absalom!* in the wink of a genius's eye. But for both Cather and Faulkner, the point of any *encounter*—in this very volume that would be renamed *Literary Encounters* for the Autograph Edition two years later in 1938—is that a lost lady such as Mrs. Fields or Rosa Coldfield could give access to the past: "At 148 Charles Street an American of the Apache period and territory could come to inherit a Colonial past" (57). Mrs. Fields is valuable because "she had a beautiful patience with Boeotian ignorance."[5] Cather humbly associates the ignorance with herself, of course.

The new "frame" for this already extant portrait of Mrs. Fields is understood to be written in the 1936 present. The fact allows Cather to make the point she has to make deftly, but firmly: she's associating the wise words of Mrs. Fields with that current writer who keeps his end up even for irreverent schoolboys. The closing statement of 1936 begins, "Today, in 1936, a garage stands on the site of 148 Charles Street" (*NUF* 73). Such desecrations have even happened since to Faulkner sites in Oxford.

Yet importantly, Cather includes in "148 Charles Street" some justification for *caring* about such a gifted writer as William Faulkner. Mrs. Fields reminisces about a Henry James work, "I do not know why success in work should affect one so powerfully, but I could have wept as I finished reading. . . . It is so difficult to do anything well in this mysterious world." Cather adds, "She rose to meet a fine performance always—to the end. At eighty, she could still entertain new people, new ideas, new forms of art" (71). Having established Mrs. Fields's insightful recognition and tolerance, Cather establishes Mrs. Fields's wisdom: "In the patriot, the philanthropist, the statesman, she could forgive abominable taste. In the artist, the true artist, she could forgive vanity, sensitiveness, selfishness, indecision, and vacillation of will. She was generous and just in her judgement of men and women because she understood Aristotle's axiom ["Virtue is concerned with action; art with production"]. "With a great gift," I once heard her murmur thoughtfully, "we must be willing to bear greatly, because it has already greatly borne" (72). I believe this speech explains Cather's willingness to hang in on the Faulkner question, that is, to bear greatly because he had greatly borne, as was self-evident to her. The statement also explains her including this essay in the collection and making it central: even in the discouraging present of 1936, as in the turning-point year of 1922 or thereabouts, she can applaud the young genius *capable* of doing things well, in this mysterious world.

About the same time *Not Under Forty* appeared, in November of 1936, Cather also received her first rejection of a story in years, "The Old Beauty," the protagonist of which is in part the negative side of her two lost ladies. But she also seemed to cheer herself up after her "winter of discontent" (Woodress 475) by going on the offensive. In the following spring she began working on her most direct fictional assault on Faulkner's world, *Sapphira and the Slave Girl*. By the time she was ready to release it four years later, she could "answer" *Absalom, Absalom!* point for point, as that novel itself answered the implied charge felt but not heard on the page in "Old Mrs. Harris" that Faulkner insufficiently understood the South.

As a group, the six essays of *Not Under Forty* speak pointedly to William Faulkner. They'll state what Cather admires, imply what she dismisses, and tell how to write great fiction. They'll try to reach him in the only way the two communicate — with literary two-by-fours. This volume is a specific encounter, a fictional contact, as well as a record of Cather's concerns. Faulkner gives every sign of understanding it very well.

"A Chance Meeting," the collection introduction, conveys a happy version of the more dour encounter fictionalized in "The Old Beauty." In its upbeat tone it is strikingly analogous to the affirmative "148 Charles Street," itself the sunny side of the more bittersweet *A Lost Lady*. It also nods admiringly to less-known works by Flaubert, who might anachronistically be said therein to display a Faulknerian imagination. In any case, "A Chance Meeting" usefully functions in this volume to describe a bossy and even dictatorial old lady who is still interesting, wise, and full of useful information. Her hardy virtue is impossible to ignore: "*Seeing things through* was evidently a habit with this old lady: witness the way she was seeing life through, going to concerts and operas in this wilting heat; being concerned that other people should go, moreover, and caring about the way in which Ravel was played, when in the course of nature her interest in new music should have stopped with César Franck, surely" (11; my italics). The point made here: listen to old ladies; they have something to show you. As an example, "I soon found that, to her, life meant just that—accomplishing things; 'doing them always a little better and better,' as she once remarked after I came to know her" (12). To judge by the simultaneous clarity and multilayered density Cather achieves in a collection of six essay reprints, this is a lesson she learned by heart. In summarizing Flaubert's niece Caro, Cather says, "she had moral qualities . . . : poise, great good sense, and a love of fairness and justice. She had the habit of searching out facts and weighing evidence, for her own satisfaction. Her speech, when she was explaining something, had the qualities of good Latin prose: economy, elegance, and exactness" (39–40). Those are also the qualities of these essays, as well as the standards these essays hold up to one who can see.

The second essay in this volume is the great "The Novel Démeublé," which deserves to be memorized by all caring students of literature. Since we are primarily concerned with Faulkner, the essay's first sentence—available to him since 1922, when it was first published in the *New Republic*—is arresting: "The novel, for a long while, has been overfurnished." Cather later adds, acknowledging surging questions about authenticity of detail and verisimilitude,

The automatic reply . . . is the name of Balzac. Yes, certainly, Balzac tried out the value of literalness in the novel, tried it out to the uttermost, as Wagner did the value of scenic literalness in the music drama. He tried it, too, with the passion of discovery, with the inflamed zest of an unexampled curiosity. If the heat of that furnace could not give hardness and sharpness to material accessories, no other brain will ever do it. To reproduce on paper the actual city of Paris [she or we might recall Jefferson or Yoknapatawpha County here]; the houses, the upholstery, the food, the wines, the game of pleasure, the game of business, the game of finance: a stupendous ambition — but after all, unworthy of an artist. In exactly so far as he succeeded in pouring out on his pages that mass of brick and mortar and furniture and proceedings in bankruptcy, in exactly so far he defeated his end. The things by which he still lives, the types of greed and avarice and ambition and vanity and lost innocence of heart which he created [and Faulkner acknowledged in his Nobel Prize Speech] — are as vital today as they were then. (46–47)

In a summary of her view of *The Scarlet Letter* within this seminal essay, Cather invites one reader of Hawthorne's *The Marble Faun* to consider *Light in August*, by way of a Hawthornian comparison: "The material investiture of the story is presented as if unconsciously; by the reserved, fastidious hand of an artist, not by the gaudy fingers of a showman or the mechanical industry of a department-store window-dresser. As I remember it, in the twilight melancholy of that book, in its consistent mood, one can scarcely ever see the actual surroundings of the people; one feels them, rather, in the dusk" (49–50). One certainly feels Hightower vividly in the dusk. And one can feel Faulkner's places as vividly as Cather's, because he has so often followed this advice.

"Miss Jewett," an essay expanded from Cather's previously published introduction to Jewett's collected stories, appropriately follows the sketch of Annie Fields, with whom Jewett, after James T. Fields's death, shared a happy "Boston marriage." In this piece Jewett makes the pronouncements Cather claims as guideposts for writing, and one must read them carefully to get them right. For example, Jewett's line, sometimes misquoted, actually reverses what one often finds on the page. It reads, "You must know the world before you can know the village" (88). Knowing the world comes first, before a wise appreciation of a small, provincial place can follow. Perhaps Faulkner was paying attention here, for in *Absalom, Absalom!* Quentin struggles valiantly to shape his story from a wider world perspective, as he cries about the South in the last line of the novel, "*I don't hate it! I don't hate it!*"

The Sarah Orne Jewett presented in this essay is "a lady, in the old high sense" (85): not a lost lady. She considered her "country friends . . . the wisest of all, because they could never be fooled about fundamentals" (86). She loved her homeplace heartily: "Every day, in every season of the year, she enjoyed the beautiful country in which she had the good fortune to be born" (87). She provokes a rule for judging: "To note an artist's limitations is but to define his talent" (81). And she is credited with the standard both Cather and Faulkner tried to observe and write by: "The design is the story and the story is the design" (77–78). The line especially helps to summarize a novel about Thomas Sutpen's design. Yet Cather, too, recognizes beyond Jewett's "individual voice" (95) the diminishing fact also key to assessing Jewett: "She was content to be slight, if she could be true" (89). Neither Faulkner nor Cather was so easily satisfied, to their greater credit.

Beyond the vibrations we recognize between Thomas Mann's prologue, quoted here, and William Faulkner's Nobel Prize speech acknowledging the human heart struggling against itself, Cather's most recent essay in this collection, on Mann's *Joseph and His Brothers*, resonates with some interestingly fierce pronouncements in the present context. Relative to her use of Phil Stone's preface to *The Marble Faun*, for example,

> The world is always full of brilliant youth which fades into grey and embittered middle age: the first flowering takes everything. The great men are those who have developed slowly, or who have been able to survive the glamour of their early florescence and to go on learning from life. . . . Yet in the very mystery lies much of the fascination which gifted young people have for their elders. (116–17)

And again,

> What we love most is not bizarre invention, but to have the old story brought home to us closer than ever before, enriched by all that the right man could draw from it and, by sympathetic insight, put into it. Shakespeare knew this fact well, and the Greek dramatists long before him. (119)

Mann's Jacob is held up as the important force in the biblical story of Joseph and his brothers; Jacob, Cather says, provides an assessing intelligence that makes the story live. Cather claims further that a story of young genius alone is not enough. We can ask, for example, who functions as the Jacob observer in *Absalom, Absalom!*—Sutpen, General Compson, Mr. Compson, or Shreve? Or is making the youngest one—Quentin—function as the oldest one the real magician's trick? Faulkner certainly seems alert to all his options after Cather remarks, "Take Jacob out of the history of Joseph, and it becomes simply the story of young genius; its cruel discipline, its ultimate triumph and worldly success. A story ever new and always gratifying, but one which never awakens the deep vibrations of the soul" (122).

The volume ends with an interesting salute to Katherine Mansfield that pairs like a bookend with "A Chance Meeting" as a sleight-of-hand magic trick. In both beginning and ending essays, we see a rather dense and slow figure whom the writer labels *myself*. That aging lady encounters another who is older and wiser than she, with lessons to teach. Relative to Katherine Mansfield, the lessons are taught by a bachelor, and they concern, not surprisingly by this point, what young writers might best do and best avoid doing. The time of the recorded encounter is 1920, but the bachelor in the center of it is about the age of Cather in 1936, when *Not Under Forty* is published. He likes early American history, Francis Parkman, and Sir George Otto Trevelyan, with all of which and whom Cather is thoroughly acquainted. The bachelor has met Katherine Mansfield as a child, has found her captivating, and then has lost interest in her work after reading "Je ne parle pas français," which offended him.

Having set up the bachelor observer for the words he can contribute to this sketch, Cather begins her summary of Mansfield as she did of Caro or Mrs. Fields or Sarah Orne Jewett. The summary anticipates the future Rosa Coldfield:

> Katherine Mansfield's peculiar gift lay in her interpretation of these secret accords and antipathies which lie hidden under our everyday behaviour, and which more than any outward events make our lives happy or unhappy. Had she lived, her development would have gone on in this direction more than in any other. When she touches this New Zealand family and those faraway memories ever so lightly, as in "The Doll's House," there is a magic one does not find in the other stories, fine as some of them are. With this theme the very letters on the page become alive. She communicates vastly more than she actually writes. (137)

The letters on the page later become alive in Rosa Coldfield's italicized chapter of *Absalom, Absalom!* because they scan in blank verse. Of course, Faulkner's magic family that Cather knows best, full of secret accords and antipathies, is the Compson family of *The Sound and the Fury*. Yet he *does* return to Quentin Compson, at this point, in *Absalom, Absalom!* Cather ends her essay on Mansfield, and her volume with its titular provocation to William Faulkner, with an image of Katherine Mansfield, the author of *Bliss*, in 1920: she "throws down her glove, utters her little challenge in the high language," and then ends "defrauded unfairly of the physical vigour which seems the natural accompaniment of a high and daring spirit" (139–40). The image seems a way of throwing down the gauntlet to William Faulkner: can you rise to this challenge of a high daring spirit expressed in high language again? That image of the gauntlet will play through her last, posthumously published book of stories, and will be associated especially with him. He picked it up, met the challenge, and recovered his high daring spirit, snatched back for himself from Hollywood's debilitations. He now completed the book many hail as his greatest, *Absalom, Absalom!*

8

Literary Hopscotch

WHEN *ABSALOM, ABSALOM!* became the final title for Faulkner's comprehensive rendition of the brave old antebellum South,
that title had a relevant biblical ring like Thomas Mann's *Joseph
and His Brothers* and an apt exclamation point like *O Pioneers!*
In this title alone, Faulkner referenced three of the five modern
writers he felt were greatest—Mann, Cather, and himself, a mu-
tinous and favored son. His elected task was to begin at the beginning, as Cather's French characters had been required to do in
Shadows on the Rock, and trace the establishment of a world, or
wrest a sustainable plantation (in New England as well as southern senses), from the wilderness.

Faulkner gives a gratuitous wave to Cather by stressing a
French element, by way of a French architect and a Creole syba-
rite, in this backwoods Mississippi jungle-swamp. They were as
factual and probable as a French element had been in Canada or
as Mexican Town had been in Cather's Red Cloud–like Colorado
of *The Song of the Lark*. Both writers were able by now to create
and justify worlds, however they liked. This novel's world, however, unlike Cather's Quebec, was thoroughly male-centered.[1]
Perhaps Faulkner insisted on that male focus so emphatically because he actually had two women he was competing with here:
Ellen Glasgow had already claimed like Balzac to have created "a

world," as "the social historian of Virginia." Cather had created another world by planting French civilization in the New World, North.[2] Faulkner needed to create a world-inclusive "design," preferably with French elements—that is, from that first gleam in a man's eye, to the last guttering moments, another century later. He wanted, like Dilsey, to see the first and the last, the beginning and the ending. He successfully accomplishes this task by showing how Thomas Sutpen first arrived to wrench Sutpen's Hundred from the wilderness, and how his last progeny finally burn with his house. In this long four-generation process Faulkner can include diverse classes, manners, races, ethnicities, lifestyles, and locales—going from country to city to foreign places, and back again.

The plot of *Absalom, Absalom!* must have riveted Willa Cather, for she carefully recapitulated it in *Sapphira and the Slave Girl*. In both novels a "masterful" planner with a life-design in mind arrives in a backwoods, wilderness area, with a band of Negro slaves utterly alien to the new terrain, and takes over land seemingly ceded by royalty (Issetibbeha for Sutpen; Lord Fairfax for Sapphira). The story's willful owner plans not only to take absolute control of the land but also to establish concomitantly a social or economic status superior to all neighbors. The character of this master-builder follows the Emersonian injunction "Build therefore your own world." It is also capricious, sometimes demonic; the builder operates formally, but only sporadically with any consideration for others. The powerful wills operating here emerge when the master planters leave an established plantation in order to build another, with maximal difficulty, in the unpromising wilderness. Thus, motivations for the building seem both to hide reasons and to flaunt intentions. For different reasons, both flee their families and then demand pride-driven and grand new lives from their wilderness. Yet, inexplicably, their accompanying slaves are loyal and numerous enough to do the job at hand. They cooperate, and accomplish their task apparently willingly, even with their own pride. The "designers" produce legitimate children, as required by their master plans. Sutpen sires Henry and Judith; Sapphira has Rachel, the youngest of her three daughters. The master planners both marry respectable plain-folk spouses, Ellen Coldfield and Henry Colbert, both of whom develop separate and irrelevant lifestyles, living largely apart from their legal mates. Each of these subordinate spouses is pious, with rule-breaking impulses traceable in their blood. The mothers in the master houses are overjoyed when their independent daughters, Judith and Rachel, receive an unexpectedly advantageous marriage proposal. After both marriages collapse, the mothers find it disconcerting to have the aging daughters near at hand. Finally, once-lovely gardens go to seed, as the caretakers age and die, or disappear. Control, in the long run, is an illusion. But the owners continue to love the designs they once realized through their own indefatigable efforts. They accept the lives they have spent realizing their designs, and sustain their distinctive characters, to the end.

Cather adopted Faulkner's plot for her last novel—lock, stock, and barrel—in order to change or adjust it (as Faulkner will change or refocus her readjusted materials, in turn). To clarify any puzzlement about fictional or marital roles, however, the Cather text's first named character, Henry Colbert, says early on to his wife, "You're the master here, and I'm the miller. And that's how I like it to be" (SSG 50). The first change involved is a reminder that *master* is not a gender-specific term. For that matter, male spouses can also be ground, as Henry James's *Portrait of a Lady* has it, "in the very mill of the conventional."

The keys to both novelists' first intentions are in their titles. The biblical story of Absalom involves brother hatred, forcing oneself on a sister, brother killing, insurrectionary moves against a father, and peremptory justice achieved after a son is left dangling by his hair. The biblical story of Ananias and Sapphira is about lying for selfish ends and being struck down for it. Cather deftly corrects Faulkner's biblical account when she reminds him that he left a detail out of his story. Subversive Absalom left a pillar, or monument, behind him to mark his own life (2 Samuel 18:18). Subversive Martin Colbert, who outraged hospitality by trying to force slave-girl Nancy, potentially his half sister, also leaves a monument for history. It is erected to mark his heroism on behalf of the insurrectionist Confederacy.

To unfold their shared plot, both Cather and Faulkner use "pictures." The builder on horseback (AA 282, 288; SSG 154) is especially memorable, as tableau requires; Sapphira, once a fine horsewoman, must in fact be *remembered* because she is no longer able to ride; Sutpen "abrupts" like a man-horse-demon (AA 8). Yet that figure of the awesome rider on a fine horse—the mythic pale horse, pale rider that Katherine Anne Porter saluted—is typical of a large number of southern fictions. The silhouette conveys control, dominance, physical skill, will, drive, speed. To do so, its horse must be enviable and the posture of the rider, arresting. Such a rider will be forceful, audacious, and arbitrary. In both these fictions the pale rider is willing to injure slaves for personal satisfactions, whether through wrestling or vicarious debauchery.

Another arresting set of pictures involves shocking "primal scenes" no observer forgets. Sutpen's wrestling half-naked and no-holds-barred with his unequal slaves, or Sapphira's abuse of her power as she leaves angry red marks with a hairbrush on the arm of her frightened slave Nancy, will serve for examples. Both character-defining pictures emphasize grossly transgressive acts of physical contact and overbearing dominance. Yet the out-of-the-box thinking we trace here in these protagonists is also present when villains perform heroically, especially during the Civil War, in battles fought off-page in remote parts of Virginia. Thomas Sutpen earns a citation for bravery and nephew Martin Colbert becomes a legend, too.

Identifying the villains in the two books is easy. Sutpen is a demon. Martin Colbert is first forecast negatively when Sapphira writes him a letter, just after vowing at her breakfast table to thwart her decent husband because he blocks her scheme to sell Nancy. She hides the letter face-down from Till, Nancy's mother, who can read. Then she goes "out" soon thereafter in her carriage, to the surprise of the household, to hand the letter personally to the postmistress. In this sequence Sapphira is suddenly called *Mrs. Colbert* five times on two pages (ssg 31–32). When our unconventional narrator stresses Sapphira's married title, she stresses her deceitfulness: biblical Sapphira drops (as Cather's Sapphira suffers dropsy) because she confirms a husband's lie. Of course, a concomitant implication is that Henry lies to himself, at least about his attitude toward Nancy, as the narrator eventually acknowledges (192–93). Connections spread and knot as they're tied down.

Many noteworthy connections between these two novels emerge from names. *Henry Colbert*, stressed as Cather's first two words, echoes two Faulkner characters, Henry Sutpen and Mr. Coldfield. Though we like Henry Colbert as we do not like Mr. Coldfield, both can be described by the same Faulkner phrase — "passive rectitude" (aa 63). Henry Sutpen is subordinate to his masterful father, Thomas, as Henry Colbert is subordinate to his masterful wife, Sapphira. Interestingly, both likeable Henry Colbert and forbidding Thomas Sutpen "talk wrong," in ways too stiff or formal to please their neighbors. The common sense declares that theirs is not "a friendly way of talking" (ssg 5). Cather returns to this subject at the end of her novel, when Nancy the slave girl returns in triumph, talking like a combination of her two formal former "masters," willful Sapphira and caring Henry, as well as the former Loudoun County British housekeeper Mrs. Machem. Obviously, Nancy has learned by way of these models and mentors how to survive with English values intact, and how to succeed and assimilate new places or roles. By the time she returns after twenty-five years, she's talking much "higher-class" than little Willa or her family. But it still doesn't seem a friendly way to talk (SSG 284). Of course, Nancy had several years more than needy young Thomas Sutpen had to absorb verbal intonations. When she left Back Creek, however, she was speaking in dialect (180, 232). Cather seems to vary the dialectal signals widely and to use the off-putting or varying verbal habits to remind her readers of a crucial truth: "Yet one must admit inconsistencies" (SSG 220). That caution is perhaps the novel's most important correction, the one Faulkner wants most to own in his own work. His immediate reply will claim it.

Faulkner's name *Rosa Coldfield* perhaps nods toward "Neighbour Rosicky" (both are sick rosies) and to the cold, sweater-hugging crone who ends buried in the cold fields in "Old Mrs. Harris." Then, nodding to the third Cather story in her 1932 volume, Faulkner has Henry Sutpen and Charles Bon ("designed" creatively through the vicarious identifications of Quentin and Shreve, their northern empathizers) recapitulate the end of "Two Friends": two very close friends argue and confront each other, a friendship shatters, after which both die badly. We thus dust the hands of *Obscure Destinies*. But we see as we do, why the impulse to redefine *Absalom, Absalom!* might press heavily upon Willa Cather.

Rosa Coldfield, enraged at her obscure destiny of being "a widow without ever having been a bride" (15), demands that attention must be paid, through her italicized chapter 5. Her arresting anger does not die, but remains "cold, implacable, and even ruthless" (10). We grant that other women whom both writers create — for example, Old Mrs. Harris, both Clytie and Judith, the women of *Sapphira* — all maintain their own and other lives through prideful acceptance of whatever must be. Rosa, conversely, cathects from "bitter undefeat" (AA 11) or "amazed outrage" (174), which makes her a thorny rose, whatever else.[3] Her black counterpart in Cather's novel also gets a chapter or book to herself: *Old Jezebel* (book 3). Jezebel is "from a fierce cannibal people" (*ssg* 91). When she is ceremoniously asked what would whet her appetite as she lies dying, Jezebel suggests "a l'il pickaninny's hand" to gnaw (89). Rosa, entering the Sutpen house violently at the end, carries a flashlight and a hatchet.

The novelistic parallels are not accidental. *Ghost* is a repeated word throughout *Absalom, Absalom!* and is initially identified with Sutpen (8), southern ladies (13), and Quentin (13). Yet *Sapphira and the Slave Girl* has ghosts, too. Tansy Dave, that "halfwitted ghost of a man" (205), seems pitiable, but not entirely unlike Sapphira's husband, Henry Colbert: "Sometimes in his sleep that preoccupation with Martin . . . came over him like a black spell" (209).

Rachel strolls in the garden with her lover, Congressman Blake, in the same way Judith strolls with Bon in their winter garden (*AA* 295). In fact, when they become the focus of male attention in both novels, Judith, Rachel, and Nancy are all in the "transitional stage between childhood and womanhood" (*AA* 67). Cather's Nancy perfectly exemplifies what Faulkner calls "the bright heels of 15 and 16" (*AA* 299) when Martin Colbert catches her in the cherry tree and holds her bare legs to his cheeks (*ssg* 180). Judith also pairs with Sapphira, for both take whatever they want, whenever they're strong enough to do so (*AA* 120). When not strong enough, they greet the world with impenetrable faces (*AA* 126; *ssg* 8).

Correspondences and anomalies occur in pairs. Mr. Compson suspects that Sutpen is actually seeking a place to hide when he arrives in Jefferson (*AA* 15), and observers think Sapphira is doing the same when she opts for Back Creek. She has been categorized as an old maid (23); so as soon as her father dies she takes a miller and runs (25), not stopping for postnuptial parties, but heading for the house she has prepared for them. In both novels, gossiping observers are mystified about how permission for the proposed marriage could have been won from the bride's father; both Coldfield and Dodderidge, however, appear to be bribable. When he arrives in Yoknapatawpha with nothing, Sutpen is twenty-five (*AA* 17); Sapphira is twenty-seven when she moves to her chosen "place of exile," but she has spent two years getting it ready (*SSG* 25), so they start at the same age. Rosa is twenty when she is outraged by Sutpen's proposal that they try to breed him a son before they wed (*AA* 19); and when Rachel is devastated by loss of husband and son, she has completed thirteen years of married life. But Rachel marries and moves out of Sapphira's clutches and to Washington when she is seventeen, about the age Rosa also moves out of her birthplace and into harm's way, to Sutpen's Hundred. "When she lay dying" is a phrase suggested in *Absalom, Absalom!* at least twice, one assumes because it brings Faulkner satisfying memories (20, 21); yet the motif is also repeated twice when Cather recounts the dying days of both Jezebel and Sapphira, both of whom lay dying in a final fashion the household remarks. In both tales, the Civil War is fought best by men with valor and strength but without pity or honor (*AA* 20; Martin qualifies). In *Absalom, Absalom!* Sutpen finally tells General Compson about his family's coming down from the western Virginia mountains when he was a lad, to go back east after his mother's death. Being insulted at a Tidewater mansion door, he develops his retaliatory life plan. Resenting the Tidewater elite, Sapphira laughs heartily over the story of an accident that defaces a pretty Tidewater girl, because "those folks from the Tidewater do hold their heads high, though I've never seen just why they feel called upon" (*SSG* 162). During the Sutpen family trek east, an unwed sister starts pregnant with one baby and ends the trip with two. In *Sapphira and the Slave Girl*, Mrs. Ringer's two daughters are both "fooled" and have illegitimate babies while living in the same western Virginia mountains Willa claims as her birthright home. The parallels suggest that both Willa and William knew something about being made to feel déclassé. The promiscuous southern mountain girl, of course, has been a popular stereotype since antebellum days, and both writers highlight it.[4]

To convey his "troubled" narration Faulkner uses italics, stressing moving thought-processes. Cather also draws attention to a very unreliable narrative voice by using grammatical slippages or archaic idioms in her all-knowing narrator's summaries (SSG 21, 22, 32, 197, 206). She too thus suggests human fallibility as a component of even the most absolutist stories — from sacred Scriptures (misquoted throughout the text) to hallowed war myths. All must be invented by human minds that provide the probability of errors and erasures as well as deliberate distortions. Both writers move here through "postmodern" relativist terrain.

Both protagonists, as master planners, learn eventually (as readers must) that personal control — especially of a text — is an illusion. All readers are reminded repeatedly that known facts are concomitantly fictions. In both master fictions, all characters, black and white, tell lies. In *Sapphira*, interestingly, the narrator — emerging as a character in book 9 — lies most brazenly. Her age is said to be "something over five" (279) when we know little Willa was nearly nine. She states in her second paragraph that "the country between Romney and Winchester had changed very little" and then promptly mentions several new brick houses with ambitious porticos that "now stood on the turnpike between Winchester and Timber Ridge" (273). Shortly after that point, she gets off a deadpan stretcher worthy of Mark Twain when she says, "The war made few enmities in the country neighbourhoods" (274). The Cather barn, Cynthia Griffin Wolff once told collected scholars in Winchester,[5] was burned by neighbors to protest the Cathers' (that is, Willa's father's family's, in contrast to her mother's family's) Yankee allegiance. In Cather's novel, the story of one exception to enmity follows, to shut off reader alarm bells. But lying is the game here, as the title's first word proclaims. We are following a liar's contest, that is, a writer's competition. As William James observed, truth is what happens to an idea. Fiction makes truth happen, and happen before your eyes, as Faulkner will shortly explain.

A major point of both novels is certainly that fictions emerge from imaginations, and that the creators necessarily conjure character, events, dialogue, and actions out of thin air—like Shakespeare's Prospero, perhaps. The point both writers concede or stress was made in previously popular local-color fiction by Richard Malcolm Johnston's Mr. Pate, who says that fiction is "a kind of a book that the half of 'em is lies, and what's more, the fellow that writ it knowed it" (187). Some truths and half-truths linger, especially in southern fictions.

After all the deliberate similarities are noted in this game we've now watched the two writers playing for nearly twenty years, the question returns, what's the point? And the point here, as it has been from the beginning, is that one writer can want to show another writer that he or she can write better his or her own way. I assume that Cather is now doing to Faulkner what she believed he'd recently been doing to her: trying to improve her material, show her how, or show her up. Once an *unmistakable pattern of imitation* can be identified, in short, the game requires finding the reversals, corrections, deliberate changes meant to do the job better. Those inversions can be as numerous as the duplications that triggered the search for them.

The most obvious changes or emendations Cather lodges about *Absalom, Absalom!* have to do with miscegenation. They are hard not to think of first, after the following passage at the end of Faulkner's greatest historical novel:

> So it's the miscegenation, not the incest, which you cant bear. . . .
> *You are my brother.*
> *No I'm not. I'm the nigger that's going to sleep with your sister. Unless you stop me, Henry.* (356–58)

Faulkner's clear point is that white men like Sutpen and Charles Bon's maternal ancestors took black women sexually, especially slaves, almost at will or random impulse—even ordered them out of the field, to meet sexual demands. Sutpen's house has his mulatto daughter, Clytie, visible to all, to remind neighbors and family that his original French-patois-speaking slaves whom he brought into Yoknapatawpha included two women for general use. Cather objects that such well-known illicit behavior, if not surprising, is still not general—at least in her part of the small-farm-owning southern country—and certainly not inevitable. It didn't *necessarily* happen that way: it just ain't necessarily so. Devout Baptist, Bible-studying Henry Colbert, for example, though living largely apart from his wife and recognizing his own randy Colbert blood, never touches Nancy, whom he loves, though he is possessive enough of her to refuse permission to sell her. Because Sapphira is jealous, she keeps Nancy within call unless her husband has decided to sleep in the master bedroom. But that act punishes Nancy for being young and desirable, not aging Henry for harboring desire.

Nancy is sexually harassed by Martin Colbert and abused by Sapphira, who designs her rape. But she is protected by the trusted head mill-hand Samson, aided to escape by Rachel, financed in fleeing by Henry, transported safely to the river by Mr. Whitford the coffin maker, and aided by good Quaker Friends to get to Canada, beyond the other shore. She is never raped, seduced, or abandoned by decent and self-respecting blacks or whites. They do mobilize slowly, but they do get her out. She gets safely to Montreal and flourishes prosperously in a British household there, where she marries and has a family. Her fortune is radically opposite Cather's forecast for a hard-working and deserving white mountain boy like Casper Flight: "A man's got to be stronger'n a bull to get out the place he was born in" (130). Cather thus emphatically disputes the "inevitable" salacious plots promising "inevitable" southern black women's rape. She thereby obviously disappoints many expectant readers and contradicts many southern white male writers. Still, by making this story "autobiographical," she claims that four generations of southern women, black and white, in her own family line, unlike the four generations of Sutpen males, confirm her more hopeful tale. The black line descends directly from Africa through Jezebel and ends with Nancy; the white one starts with Sapphira and ends with little Willa of the coda, who signs off by name and in person.

All of the women in this four-generation story, white and black, suffer terrible hardships. Till's mother, in fact, burns to death in an accident witnessed by her traumatized little daughter, who almost loses her power of speech. Till must be taken in by the compassionate British housekeeper Mrs. Machem, and nurtured in the big house at Chestnut Hill. Once ensconced at Back Creek, Sapphira trades a stable boy for her, after Till reaches the transformative fairy-tale age of fifteen (Callandar 35–36). Jezebel the foremother has survived the middle passage chained naked on deck; Till survives "a lifelong sentence," as Harry Gordon of *Lucy Gayheart* called it, lovelessly married by Sapphira to a "capon man." She is impregnated—her miscegenation is by her own choice—by a white man passing through, who is so unknown he's identified with both Baltimore (9) and Cuba (69, 72). And Nancy must be sent to a foreign land because her beloved home is unsafe. All these lives are hard, but none involves inevitable rape.

Furthermore, the white women fare scarcely better than the slaves. Sapphira has lost the health that allowed her to supervise and manage her affairs, to be herself. Rachel has lost her reason for living, along with her idolized husband for whom she "slaved herself" and the son she worshiped. Prepubescent Molly has lost her sister Betty and nearly her own life through diphtheria. And little Willa seems none too well herself, not even allowed out of bed to greet Nancy. None escape hardships, horrors, changes, and frights. Yet Cather insists that these bad things do not include "inevitable" unwanted sexual penetration as a predictable part of all female, and especially all black female, life. This is a woman's version of history, not a man's, and gender makes a difference in perspective. *Male-identified* Sapphira's mistake is to assume the inevitability of rape. Isolated Sapphira fails to calculate female solidarity and ingenuity into her schemes.

In one subtext, however, Cather seems to ask whether this chaste escape is any more improbable than another story we love, *The Wizard of Oz*. As a consistently observed inconsistency, Nancy seems to travel with the same metaphoric company Dorothy moves with, along her yellow brick road. If Dorothy can blow out of Kansas and then return safely to the comforts of home while all cheer, why not Nancy? The deceptive narrator provides Nancy with Dorothy's endearing impediments: overpowering fear, like the cowardly lion; no heart for the task, like the tin man; and no head for planning, like the scarecrow. "I been kind-a flighty in the head like," Nancy says to excuse her behavior. Rachel surveys the frightened woman and "could feel the courage oozing out of the girl beside her" (236). Nancy so loses heart as she crosses the Potomac that she shivers, falls silent, and cannot even speak to say goodbye or thank you (235). If Faulkner can do it, why not I? the narrator seems provoked to challenge. *I* at least use a familiar story line when I start the journey. In fact, as most recognize, she also most pointedly throws in *Uncle Tom's Cabin* while she's at it. Volumes of slave narratives issued by the Smithsonian are not less improbable. And as Faulkner will shortly point out, "What the heart holds to becomes truth, as far as we know truth" (GDM 284).

The male writer's key phrase in these books is *victorious dust*; the woman's is *plucky survival*. In this comparison the man's men are heroic and doomed; the woman's women are stealthy and productive. The man's writer stresses courage and fatality; the woman's, sympathy and resilience. Little Willa, like Quentin, is just trying to unfold, make up, or piece together the crazy quilt of her main story with whatever patches come to hand. She wants it to cover her own vision. Her story as she recalls it, however, is aided by her white parents and grandmother, who join black Till in lionizing Nancy for escaping. All joyously welcome Nancy home, which triumphant journey Nancy can afford to finance herself, as they apparently could not. Victorious Nancy is our hero; angry Sapphira is our protagonist. Both are equally important and both are human: they have their inconsistencies and we observe them.

That need brings us to the other most obvious difference Cather chooses for her own version of southern history. Cather is always clear but never simple. Her aim is to tell the story plainly, but with the reverberating overtones or complexity to meet her own intelligent standards, while keeping what's going on in full sight always. The complexity is hidden under her calm surfaces, not signaled in crashing waves as if a hurricane were moving over. Some like the drama of storms, some like the chance to see to the bottom when they remember to look. And when Faulkner chooses to show he can play Cather's game by trumping her seven spades with seven no-trump, in *The Reivers*, the lovers of crashing turbulence sing out that they prefer the roar of the breakers, like Cather's Thea Kronborg.

One way Cather accomplishes her goals is to clearly identify and equalize her two female antagonists in her title, *Sapphira and the Slave Girl*. Then she goes back further than Faulkner's 1833 start, to the capture, transport, and sale of Jezebel. Jezebel is the first survivor whose resulting power of will lets her "lord it over" slackards she disapproves of, such as lazy Manuel, in whose pants she'd like to sew dock burs.[6] Such willful pride has also led Jezebel to become a head gardener equal to or surpassing Sapphira. Like Candide, the women here learn to tend their house and chop their wood and make their gardens grow. As their opposite, Sutpen "tore [his garden] violently" out of virgin land. Wild Jezebel adds years to Cather's version and its accumulating "authority," its claim to be more complete. To this claim, Faulkner reacted immediately.

In stressing that the narrative is validated by an eavesdropping *child* who is something over five, but clearly an unreliable hearer and recorder, Cather asks a reader to keep in an *adult* mind several differences with *Absalom, Absalom!* Faulkner's eavesdropper is a much older Rosa Coldfield, who still can't get all her details straight; the Back Creek adults, not unlike Mr. Compson, also have their own versions of the story and are also inclined to censor it before it reaches the ears of little Willa. Only by remaining quiet does she encourage them to forget her, or forget that she's a little pitcher with big ears. When Till tells her stories to little Willa, she tells them differently every time, to the child's delight. But the stress is on factual slippage and variation. Like Quentin and Shreve's speculations in their dormitory room, the resulting story changes, refocuses, means something different with every telling: that's history for you, not to mention fiction. The story Willa the narrator tells has the grammatical flaws, quaint idioms, lapses and gaps, convenient smudges, of overheard narratives told by fallible sources. This version of history, it appears, is what both writers acknowledge. Histories depend on the appeal of conclusions they are *designed* to convey. Histories are *designs*, like lies.

Here are some of Cather's carefully designed conclusions. Her rule about writing fiction is articulated by Mrs. Machem: "there was all the difference in the world between doing things exactly right and doing them somehow-or-other" (71). Till infers from this rule that it's the devil's voice that whispers to relax, or rush through. Cather's application of the rule requires her to point out—telling the truth but telling it slant—that she's going to tell a story about southern history, which will necessarily be a story put together out of the stretchers told by liars; her design requires naming a liar in the title's first word, and resorting to the chuckles of a liar at her end, by closing *with a paragraph in italics* (italics such as we find in Rosa's chapter). She then signs it with her name—throws a gauntlet. In between title and last paragraph, however, the print doesn't wiggle but comes out straight-faced, as we might say, while it serves her purposes, her design. Apparently, that italicized coda *was* her final flourish, added to the end after she had completed the corrected draft of her typed manuscript, now housed coda-less as preface-less, in the Drew University library. One missing manuscript may be assumed to have intervened as printer's copy between the typescript now at Drew and the final printed page. We may infer that that printer's copy put the italicized coda last, as Cather's last decision about her novel. Those italics really were chosen to be the last stroke.

Cather structures this novel with exceptional care. That care allowed Faulkner to zoom in on book 2, "Nancy and Till," about slaves. Cather here answers the question, "Why is Mr. Compson working so hard in *Absalom, Absalom!* to arrange Rosa Coldfield's story? Why must it make sense to him, especially after Rosa has designated her story as Quentin's problem? Quentin is his son; but Nancy is Till's daughter. Till sits on her cabin steps "watching the long twilight coming on" (68),[7] after Sapphira and Nancy have left for Winchester. Till tries to understand why Sapphira has chosen Nancy for the Easter trip instead of herself. She even gets up at one point and goes in the cabin for a shoulder quilt, interrupting her meditations as Mr. Compson interrupts his reflections to get a cigar. The narrator goes on to tell us that Till preferred to live "among 'folks'" (69), and her kind of folks are not available to her this side of Winchester: "Deep in her heart Till felt slighted and left behind" (68). We infer, as Faulkner might, that Cather thinks one might want to explain such sustained talk as Mr. Compson's by assuming the thinker who liked living among "folks" is jealous of his child. He talks long and hard to digest the fact that Quentin has been invited into an action that he has been left out of. Till would know just how he feels. Both parents are jealous of their children, as Sutpen may be also. But it's really Mr. Compson's own condition that produces the story he thinks out. So Cather interprets *Absalom, Absalom!* in *Sap-*

phira and the Slave Girl just as Faulkner interpreted *Death Comes for the Archbishop* in *The Sound and the Fury*.

Then there's this matter of incest, certainly a central issue in the stories featuring Quentin. Cather allows Sapphira to joke insultingly of incest to her husband, Henry, when she pricks him by asking whether he has a "family feeling" about Nancy. Nancy's paternity, Sapphira inserts, has been "fixed on" either Henry's brother Jacob or Guy (9). Jacob may be an arbitrarily chosen name, but it also recalls the literary encounters over Mann's *Joseph and His Brothers*. Jacob used a substitute wife while working to earn his beloved Rachel—which is also the name of Sapphira's daughter. In any case, the immediately planted suggestion about Nancy's Colbert paternity places Henry under suspicion for incestuous feelings. Innuendo compounds the errors for which Sapphira wishes to prod Henry and instill guilt. And when Martin Colbert is invited on the scene to debauch Nancy in one way or the other, he too is an incest suspect: Nancy could be his half sister. Literally laidback little Willa, embedded in this story review, seems to say, We can deal with incest in this southern fiction—by southern standards, mere child's play. What we deny is *fated* victimization. Nancy is not going to end in my story, as Milly Jones's mother did, in a Memphis or Montreal brothel. It's not going to happen that way here, because in my story women are going to prevent it. The good folks are just not going to stand for it, even if wicked Sapphira (my great-grandmother and progenitress, who defined my own wicked bloodline) just might have enjoyed it. I myself still chuckle over all those stories. And I'm admitting it *in italics*: these are not matters of lapsed courage, but of willed choice.

James Early's study *The Making of Go Down, Moses* helps to clarify such facts as that the short story "The Bear" was printed independently, in the shorter version that omits section 4, the day after the novel that includes section 5 was published in 1942. The printing history reminds us a bit of *Obscure Destinies*. The penultimate part of "The Bear," published two years after *Sapphira and the Slave Girl*, was that infamous section 4, so meticulously parsed by Godden and Polk. This section contains one sentence of 16,000 words, a six-page sentence designed to summarize southern history. Faulkner cautioned editor and printer not to change a letter or punctuation mark of it, and Early considers "this section . . . the genealogical and emotional center of *Go Down, Moses*" (40). Faulkner then printed "The Bear," without section 4, in *The Big Woods* (1955). Nestrick comments that section 4 seems to thumb a nose at critics who insist on differences between author and narrator, and even between characters who ought to be clearly differentiated. That's a nose-thumbing like the one at the end of *Sapphira and the Slave Girl*.

We are now aware that all those section 4 results—a summary of southern history, a deliberate fuzzing of differences between author and narrator, and a blurring of lines between characters who are also blended by bloodline—occurred two years earlier in *Sapphira and the Slave Girl*. While *Sapphira* was Cather's answer to *Absalom*, section 4 of "The Bear" appears to be Faulkner's hastily and impulsively written answer to *Sapphira*. The speed of his reply, however, still does not indicate whether his response was negative or positive. He could have been exhilarated by her recognitions, her acknowledgment of his power and importance. He could have written section 4 to salute her and agree with her, albeit or necessarily in his own most idiosyncratic style.

Section 4 starts with two males "juxtaposed" (a Cather word) in a commissary. Though a commissary-like building can still be visited on Faulkner's old Greenfield farm near Oxford, the commissary also duplicates the mill room Cather describes, in which Henry Colbert sleeps and keeps his accounts in *Sapphira* (47–48). In both confined spaces, as Faulkner and Cather describe them, the central objects of importance are the business desk and the ledgers. In Cather's less-well-known but first-written version, "His 'secretary' was also of chestnut. . . . It was both writing-desk and bookcase. Above the desk four shelves held ledgers and account books—and a curious assortment of other books as well" (48). The first time we see Henry alone, it is "one rainy March day about four o'clock in the afternoon . . . [when] the miller was sitting at his secretary, going through his ledger. His purpose was to check off the names of debtors to whom he would not, under any circumstances, extend further credit. He found so many of these names already checked once, and even twice, that after frowning over his accounts for a long while, he leaned back in his chair and rubbed his chin" (48–49). While the first part of *Sapphira* that Faulkner decides to focus on is the miller, the miller is also the character Cather recommends to his attention in her first two words. Once again, Faulkner reads significantly better and more perceptively than most Cather students. Henry Colbert can no more make his names and facts respectable than can Uncle Buck and Uncle Buddy. In no fictions do the ledgers add up reasonably. Ike then, like Henry, pores over the discrepancies desperately, but can do nothing with them until he accounts for inconsistencies, as Cather has advised.

What is most arrestingly redundant, however, is the early emphasis in both books on the four generations that have created these accounts (SSG 8; GDM 4:245). The four generations supply the authority—in both cases. Blotner helpfully reminds us that the Oxford newspapers were stressing four generations of Falkners just at the time that William was writing "The Bear" (2:1080). Their focus, however, was on Johncy's new novel, not the prodigal elder brother, who is being required at the moment to relinquish his position in local attention. In any case, both Cather and Faulkner seem to say in these parallel fictions that this is the way it was in the South, and four generations of my family, white and black, have witnessed to me that it is so. Faulkner's last addition to *Go Down, Moses* was his dedication to Mammy Callie, Caroline Barr, his Till-equivalent.

The first inferences to emerge from the McCaslin ledgers, as at least four generations of Faulkner readers have witnessed, concern miscegenation and incest. Old LCQ McCaslin, the apparently wicked grandfather of childless Ike, apparently bought and bedded the slave Eunice and then, after two years of sexual usage, married her off to Thucydes. Their child, Tomasina, is acknowledged by Ike to be McCaslin's daughter. When she is grown and becomes entangled with her master and father, the imagined start of their involvement duplicates Nancy's care of the mill room: "Perhaps he had sent for her at first out of loneliness, to have a young voice and movement in the house, summoned her, bade her mother send her each morning to sweep the floors and make the beds and the mother acquiescing since that was probably already understood, already planned" (sec. 4: 258). When Tomey is already three months pregnant by her father and after the incestuous pregnancy begins to show, Eunice drowns herself in the pond, as Nancy threatened to do. Ike's only defense—"There must have been love" (258)—is Cather's only defense of the miscegenation that produced Nancy. Both plots concede that attractive female slaves are the prey of white male sexual predators.

Both section 4 and *Sapphira* also confirm a somewhat lighter side to slavery. At least until he lost his sweetheart, Sapphira's slave Dave freely courted a receptive lass visiting nearby; in fact, he "renamed himself," as did both Wilella Cather and William Falkner. Dave rolled in a tansy bed so that he would smell sweet as he went courting and became thereby "Tansy Dave." That he was one of the merriest and most talented musicians on Sapphira's farm before he turned luckless in love makes Sapphira sympathetic. Thereafter, Dave is allowed to wander unpursued while hunting, armed with arms-owning mill-hand Sampson's borrowed gun. Sapphira's forbearance is part of the Virginia picture as Uncle Buck and Uncle Buddy's unconventional arrangement with their slaves is part of the Mississippi lore.

Renaming focuses Faulkner's wilder comic inventions about Percival Brownlee. We could if we wished, however, pick up an overtone heard but not seen on the page here in reference to Cather's and Wagner's and literary myth's *Parsifal*, the holy fool who also soundtracks through *One of Ours*. Unlike Parsifal, Percival is effeminate and corrupt; but like Parsifal, he is incompetent. As useless property, he's as detestable to the Buck and Buddy who converse through ledgers as Fat Lizzie and Bluebell are to Henry Colbert. When he displays no ascertainable skill or use, costs them more and more money, and won't leave any more willingly than Lizzie and Bluebell, Uncle Buck and Uncle Buddy argue in writing in the ledgers about what to do. He is an intractable problem. Their solution: *rename him*. That is perhaps a wise, as well as a comic, gambit.

The lax supervision of slaves, of course, runs through all these tales from *Absalom, Absalom!* to *Sapphira and the Slave Girl* to section 4. It culminates most amusingly, to my mind, in the story of Uncle Buck and Uncle Buddy, who herd their slaves into the big house at sundown, nail the front door shut, and never glance at the back. Their gentleman's agreement is that no questions will be asked so long as all slaves are present behind the front door at sunrise. Faulkner's joke nevertheless confirms Cather's statement that the elements necessary to an underground railroad are present in Back Creek, but no slave before Nancy has ever needed to run away. When Nancy disappears, Sapphira is far too proud to send slave catchers after her; she merely figures out who helped, and then exiles Rachel. Merry Tap, Sapphira's favorite male slave, has made naughty jokes to her with impunity and waited on her like a royal courtier. He is trusted and able to ride to Winchester on Henry's best horse, to fetch Dr. Clavenger when the grandchildren are sick; Clytie is trusted and able to go for Charles Bon's son in New Orleans. Both slaves are trusted because they trust themselves to do the job right. But the serious side of both these stories still recognizes slave incarceration in the master's house; that's where Sapphira has Nancy imprisoned in the hall outside her own door.

In describing history, both *Sapphira* and "The Bear's" section 4 underscore fluid answers to the question, Whose history is it, anyway? That is, who is the hero and who is the protagonist? The answer always depends on who's telling the story, but the fictions concede that you can't always tell the tellers apart. Under these circumstances, one also cannot separate author and narrator, whatever the official academic rules declare. Neither writer tries. Both call attention to opposite facts. Both almost ostentatiously misquote sacred scriptures as they recount lies (sec. 4: 249). Faulkner, as Cather, defines liar and human as synonyms (249). Both acknowledge that slavery is wrong and that the land that permits it is subject to misfortune. Both agree that *freedom* is elusive, if not nonexistent, and that the *hero* can be the one who endures long enough to learn pity, humility, pride. And finally, after all is said and done, Cather's is still a female story and Faulkner's is still a male story. When one is measuring constructions — artworks, histories, and lies — gender can make a very substantial difference.

9

Crossing the Finish Lines

WHEN CATHER DESIGNED her posthumous volume of short stories, she planned to undermine her prominent female rivals in her first story, review her own career in her second, and summarize her adult conversations with William Faulkner in the third and last—her final word to him and to all. I have described the book's first two stories elsewhere.[1] We return in this chapter to that final story because it substantially affected Faulkner and elicited *The Reivers*. Cather's compacted and exact final sentence, in which she really does get it all between one cap and one period, is certainly funnier when one has recently been pondering the six-pager of "The Bear's" section 4:

> "Anyhow, when that first amphibious frog-toad found his water-hole dried up behind him, and jumped out to hop along till he could find another—well, he started on a long hop."

Reading merrily or not, we note that Cather does not intend to be outdone by time, this time. She starts that final sentence with a casual "Anyhow" before moving back to that first amphibious frog-toad preceding mammals. We also note the *fours* that keep reappearing in both writers' works: four lines, four generations to give authority, forefathers and grandparents, four sections.

Cather inserts into her concluding story another resonating four: an allusion to Shakespeare's *Henry IV* that seems uncommonly reverberant. It was a challenge, and Faulkner, as we would expect, rose to it. Our initial task is to consider new aspects of "Before Breakfast."

First, Cather lets Faulkner know that she's noticed more than *Mosquitoes*. She says that her story's protagonist, after glimpsing a young woman taking a dip in the icy North Atlantic, "scolded her ghost all the way home" (165), as the Compsons scolded Rosa Coldfield and her ghosts in *Absalom, Absalom!* She says her protagonist was, in fact, a frail man who made it up to himself by going hunting, an apparent nod to the various hunting trips as well as the hunting stories of *Go Down, Moses*. In fact, Grenfell's greatest trophy is a white bear from Labrador, which reminds us of Faulkner's black bear, whitewashed. But when Cather's protagonist starts a vacation by packing Shakespeare's *Henry IV*, I realize that *he*, at least, plans to read it, in contrast to Hightower of *Light in August*, who put away his Tennyson to read "food for a man," *Henry IV*, only to fall asleep without, one infers, absorbing much (LA 353). Potential lessons and inferences now follow.

But first, Cather also nods toward early works, as well as later ones or the famous ones. She recognizes *Soldier's Pay* by having the protagonist belong to a law firm named Grenfell and Saunders, Bonds. Saunders is Cecily's last name in *Soldier's Pay*,[2] and *Bonds* cocks an eyebrow at Jim Bond of *Absalom, Absalom!* In fact, the one syllable *Bonds* recalls all the back-and-forthing about slavery, freedom, and responsibility in all those historical fictions by both of them, and rope-ties protagonist Henry Grenfell—that is, puts him in bonds—besides. Cather lets Faulkner know she sees *all* he wrote. Her manner is not unlike parental spelling out of important messages over the heads of preliterate three-year-old listeners: ourselves.

It's what else she does besides summarize Faulkner's work by deft allusions (as she has done her own work in the preceding story, "The Best Years," or he has done hers in *As I Lay Dying*) that interests us. For example, I'm arrested by the name *Henry Grenfell* itself. The surname sounds to me like a surly churl who's lost his grin (*i*'s and *e*'s sound alike in many southern dialects), or like a slurred reference to Faulkner's Greenfield Farm. But the *Henry* gets down to business. After we recall Henrys Sutpen and Armstid, Colbert and Seabury (in "The Old Beauty"), Eastman ("Consequences"), not to mention Harry Gordon from *Lucy Gayheart* and Uncle Harry of "Uncle Valentine," we're prepared for comprehensive possibilities implicating both writers. I think the point forming is bigger than random Henrys in their parts of American fiction; Cather makes sure she focuses attention when she has Henry Grenfell pack that *Henry IV, Part 1*, and then bristle about it. If she has gauntlets on her mind for this last volume, as it seems she does after having Evangeline Knightly (named the good-message defender) start "The Best Years" wearing them, she pulls one off to throw down here. A gauntlet lands before Faulkner in her last—and also summarizing—story. It is almost as if Cather were playing the role of gauntlet-throwing Bolingbroke at the start of *Richard II*. That metaphor or allusion to gauntlets is one Faulkner will pick up and correct, as she did his omission of Absalom's pillar in *Sapphira and the Slave Girl*. His picking up the Bolingbroke gauntlet also initially sets Faulkner up as Bolingbroke's heir, the young misbehaving Prince Hal. His novel to come will include the phrase "the knightly shapes of my male ancestors" (*Reivers* 51). Hal must learn to be king, of course, but he eventually seizes the crown, even in Shakespeare.

Willa does not go gently into that good night. What she accomplishes in her last printed story written on her way out is fully up to her own highest standards. We must proceed slowly if we are to appreciate this consummately subtle performance. It starts with a quick scene and a throwaway allusion. Harrison, Henry's son, has entered Grenfell's bedroom and interrupted his father's packing for a vacation his family resents because he plans to spend it alone.

> On top of his pyjamas and razor case lay two little books bound in red leather. Harrison picked up one and glanced at the lettering on the back.
>
> *King Henry IV, Part I.*
>
> "Light reading?" he remarked. Grenfell was stung by such impertinence. He resented any intrusion on his private, personal, non-family life.
>
> "Light or heavy," he remarked dryly, "they're good company. And they're mighty human."
>
> "They have that reputation," his son admitted.
>
> A spark flashed into Grenfell's eye. Was the fellow sarcastic, or merely patronizing?
>
> "Reputation, hell!" he broke out. "I don't carry books around with my toothbrushes and razors on account of their reputation."
>
> "No, I wouldn't accuse you of that." The young man spoke quietly, not warmly, but as if he meant it. He hesitated and left the room. (153–54)

But in this last thunderously resonating literary reference, which reminds us that every Cather fiction has carried a buried allusion to Shakespeare, we sense other reverberations and flourishes. For a fact, she gets in three Shakespearean plays as possible referents, for the space it takes to name one: because *Henry IV, Part 1* can pair plausibly with either *Richard II*, whose plot leads up to it, or *Henry IV, Part 2*, which follows it up. In this story Grenfell has packed "two little books bound in red leather" that seem to match (153), but which two are they? It's a three-plays-for-one-title maneuver, Cather's typical kind of "suggestiveness."

Henry Grenfell's name certainly suggests Shakespeare's troubled Henry IV, formerly Harry Bolingbroke, whose grin fell away when as a young man he was crowned King of England in *Richard II*. Cather's Grenfell was equally young when he collided with his destiny. Since Cather's allusion initially concerns the personalities of the analogous Henrys—Grenfell and the imminent Henry IV—she initially draws more from *Richard II*: here uncrowned Bolingbroke plays foil to King Richard. In Cather's story young Grenfell clerks for the most conservative law firm in Colorado until he becomes such a success that he gets himself into Bonds, a life that leaves him with a "hair-trigger stomach."

Cather's underscored doubleness of vision here follows Shakespeare's example: there will be two kings at the beginning and end of this three-play sequence, plus two Harry juniors, Hal and Hotspur. Even in Shakespeare's play the father-son relationship is labeled *punishing*.[3] Besides his son Harrison, Henry Grenfell also has two other sons, one said to be as brilliant as Harrison is. But we don't know which of the other two is distinguished because she never names the others, as she never names the other Shakespeare play. Doubleness of vision is the established norm. Cather may be saluting Faulkner as an equal here, but she's also giving notice that she's not throwing in the towel; she's leaving open the question of who is the rightful royal ruler. Beyond asking this challenging question, she's throwing that *gauntlet*, the kind that dominant master riders wear, the kind they weave fictions around. She further alludes here to a Shakespearean saga that begins with old John of *Gaunt*, time-honored Lancaster, the same name and line Myra Henshawe murmured as she lay dying in *My Mortal Enemy*, where we learned that lovers can be enemies, too.[4] We have not yet begun to fight.

At the beginning of "Before Breakfast," Cather's now-elderly Grenfell prepares to go on vacation and enjoy alone his "glorious loneliness" (159). But he faces on his first vacation morning the same problems that haunted Shakespeare's Henry IV: how to imagine the undisturbed possession of a beloved island that he has learned is foundationally divided; and how to love a first son and heir whose values, interests, and manners seem utterly alien to him. After dyspeptic fuming, Henry rediscovers a welcome fire in the belly as he smells the coffee, passes from shade to sunshine, recognizes a zest in his morning, and gets his appetite and digestion back.[5] What has transformed Grenfell's outlook is his seeing a plucky young person perform a chosen task under hard circumstances, without dodging. What stands out to us, however, is that the young person is female. Grenfell started his vacation day by fulminating about the planet Venus. Then he sees her avatar and it perks him up immensely.

Grenfell returns to his cabin to find approvingly that his man "William hadn't waited; he was wisely breakfasting" (166). Assuming for the moment that Grenfell first signified the elder Willa when annoyed with a younger version of her "line," the question that now arrives as the story ends is, which William is Cather referencing here, Shakespeare or Faulkner? It seems one of her clearest ambiguities. Faulkner, however, might have been flattered. Even if William is a "man Friday" who is "boarded out" with a fisherman's family as befits one subservient to Henry (159), he's also named, by allusions in the story, alongside Shakespeare. And this William is not waiting deferentially, but has gone ahead and started to eat with a heartier appetite than Grenfell normally enjoys. No wonder Cather's posthumous volume was in Faulkner's library at the time of his death! In contrast to this story's William, kinglike Grenfell, like Henry IV, has been given a feast by Fortune and then deprived of the stomach to enjoy it (*Part 2*, 4.4.103–7). Grenfell and Bolingbroke have both paid dearly for their achievements, after which they are defined by restless nights and bitter dawns. In Grenfell's recognition, "The bitter truth was that his worst enemy was closer even than the wife of his bosom — was his bosom itself!" (156). Like Richard II before Henry IV, Grenfell chides himself.

"Before Breakfast," with the help of its Shakespeare allusions, focuses on the problem that has kept Grenfell awake his first night on the island: how to relax on an island composed of halves from different periods that have emerged from disparate foundations.

> This royal throne of kings, this scept'red isle,
> This earth of majesty, this seat of Mars,
> This other Eden, demi-paradise,
> This fortress built by Nature for herself . . .
> This blessed plot, this earth, this realm, this England.
>   (2.2.31–50)

Cather seems to echo Gaunt's words when she describes Grenfell's island:

> England, bound in with the triumphant sea
> Whose rocky shore beats back the envious siege
> Of wat'ry Neptune, is now bound in with shame,
> With inky blots and rotten parchment bonds.
> That England that was wont to conquer others
> Hath made a shameful conquest of itself.
>   (2.2.61–66)

Cather's story asks, with the help of her allusion to Shakespeare, how anyone lives with two chiefs in one territory. We recall that Cather resorts to making autobiographical allusions for those characters who must perform her most dangerous, or nervous-making, tasks. The Shakespeare allusion, in turn, helps this story to puzzle out how a power figure might tolerate an irritating successor? how far should manners be expected to go? As *Richard II*–quoting Myra Henshawe says, "It's all very well to tell us to forgive our enemies; our enemies can never hurt us very much. But oh, what about forgiving our friends? . . . that's where the rub comes!" (*spow* 554).[6] What, in fact, is worth atoning for, and what is worth celebrating? Leaving as wide open as possible that question about who one's mortal enemy might be on such a little postage stamp of an island, whether it might be one's own bosom as Grenfell's is, and whether there's any significant difference between what one loves most and what one fears most — questions robustly active in Shakespeare's trilogy about Henry IV — we turn to other Shakespearean resonances in "Before Breakfast."

Cather seems to ask, is this Henry now before us a king, a rascal, or a clown? Sticking to literature, Henry Grenfell, like King Henry IV, has reached the pinnacle of his power at Grenfell and Saunders, Bonds, by accident. The "firm truth," however, can be interpreted two ways: it's a businesslike way to identify Faulkner as the prototype for Grenfell; it's a metaphoric way to assume he's one of two bonded and equal partners. In either case, Grenfell, like Bolingbroke, once collided with another who was coasting, rose from his spill to rescue something important thereby, gained the favor of the powerful, and thus found glory. In his successful life Grenfell, as did Bolingbroke, has paid the bills of his expensive family but has come to look suspiciously on relatives and former friends. Yet from the first he has also displayed an occasional and quixotic willingness to forgive his enemies. He is now himself a loner, like Henry IV, envious of his opponents' preferable children, and anxious about what his own sons "just reach out and *take*" (152) with no struggle (as Hal reaches to take the crown at the end of *Henry IV, Part 2*, when he thinks his father is dead). Grenfell's self-congratulatory regard for the way he worked hard to gain his kingdom also seems defensively smug and potentially self-deceptive. We know him to be smart, ambitious, inconsistent, and energetic, but not necessarily trustworthy. It is therefore gratifying to see him regain some faith in the younger generation and their future, as Henry IV does at the end of both parts of *Henry IV*.

Yet Henry Grenfell also seems Cather-like. He owns a cabin that looks like Cather's, on an island in the North Atlantic very like her beloved Grand Manan. Here he, as she, loves to isolate himself and take long walks along nearby trails. The most obvious walking path leads by waterfalls, as two busloads of Cather scholars discovered for themselves by visiting the island in 1995. Once his eyes are open, Grenfell observes the primary things that seem Cather signatures. For example, her primary colors appear: a "high red cliff overhanging the sea" (149); "new-born light, yellow as gold" (160); blue shades and "indigo blue" water (142). We also recognize the basic sexual facts Cather often represents through anatomized landscapes or metaphors: an ejaculatory waterfall that "leaped hundreds of feet over the face of the cliff and fell into the sea" (162) and a nymph that opens and shuts her shell like a clam before swimming out to the rocks. Grenfell thus begins to seem a lot like one of those autobiographical males in Cather's work: Jim Burden, Niel Herbert, Godfrey St. Peter, possibly even Bartley Alexander. We therefore allow ourselves to ask, is Grenfell supposed to suggest only Faulkner sifted through Shakespeare, or is he also a surrogate for Cather, too? Is she managing three references for the space of one, as she did with those plays? Or does Grenfell represent all the driven and successful businessfolk who write for money, for their living? Nobody around here seems to be relinquishing any inheritance for a life in the wilderness, as did Ike McCaslin in "The Bear." And is this valued and glorious loneliness the thing all must come to in the end, not unlike Jean Latour in *Death Comes for the Archbishop*? Who or what *is* this newly imagined Henry? Is his crown, his kingly dominance as sole owner and proprietor of this little postage stamp of soil that seems to him a demi-paradise and blessed plot, worth fighting over?

In any case, Shakespeare's *Henry IV* offers transferable images that reappear in Cather's text. In the first lines of Shakespeare's play we glimpse King Henry IV looking for "frighted peace" with "opposed eyes . . . like the meteors of a troubled heaven," while he feels "shaken" and "wan with care." His hope is to "March all one way and be no more oppos'd / Against acquaintance, kindred, and allies." In the first parallel, as well as story scene, we glimpse Grenfell after his sleepless night with his head and eyes tipped upside down to receive eye drops, from which odd posture he soon wonders whether he has treated his family exactly right—just like Henry IV. Yet he resents the family because his wife and eldest son seem "a close corporation" (154), much as the Duke of York's wife and son comically incorporate their efforts at the end of *Richard II* to extract a pardon from Bolingbroke for the treason of which York accuses his son (5.3). We have watched Grenfell create a case against his son, too. Grenfell especially resents the fact that his sons don't chase the ball but reach out and take it with fine hands, as *both* Bolingbroke does in *Richard II* and Hal does in *Henry IV, Part 2*. Grenfell's bitterness toward professors and physicists in "Before Breakfast" parallels Henry IV's bitterness before his death at the public failure to recognize the terrible effects on one's health of being a self-made king and of wearing a crown. The "intestine shock" Henry registers in the opening scene of *Part 1* reflects Grenfell's "hair-trigger stomach." At the least, Professor Fairweather's name is as transparent as Shakespeare's Shallow, Pistol, Silence, or Wart from *Part 2*. And Grenfell's recognition that his "worst enemy" is "his bosom itself" corresponds to Henry IV's similar recognition at the end of *Part 2* (4.5.182–220). Henry IV calls his son Hal "my nearest and dearest enemy" (*Part 1*, 3.3.123).

With his head awry, before breakfast, Grenfell spots the planet Venus. This glimpse of the morning star, however, follows his sight of the "big snowshoe hare" he remembers fondly from two years before. The hare reminds us of "hare-brained Hotspur" (*Part 1*, 5.2.19), whom the king admires, as well as the reluctance to "start a hare" (*Part 1*, 1.3.197–98). Hotspur's remark that it's easier to "pluck honor from the pale-faced moon, / Or dive into the bottom of the deep" (*Part 1*, 1.3.202–3) frames the sky-to-sea survey Grenfell accomplishes here, but reminds us that his tale begins after a troubled night of sleepless agitation because a geologist has told him the two ends of his preferred world are different from each other. Grenfell soon doffs his "easy robes of peace" (*Part 1*, 5.1.13), in this story his "eiderdown bathrobe" (158), to dress for action that commences with the dawn, as does the battle between Henry IV and Hotspur. But after all the parallels are noted, the main point is that Grenfell is an "unthankful king" of the island (*Part 1*, 1.3.136) and a "forgetful man" (*Part 1*, 1.3.161), whose former allies cannot trust him. Cather seems willing to let us make the charges against both Faulkner and herself. They are the two disparate halves of a literary kingdom who emerge from different periods but now have no choice but to stick it out together for "the eternities" (148; a Faulkner word), or at least for a long time (a Cather recalculation). Cather concedes in this last public moment that they are bonded.

In the role of Fairweather, Cather permits herself to tell Faulkner what he probably doesn't want to hear. Faulknerian Grenfell, of course, "always liked to talk about [his special place] to the right person. At first he thought Professor Fairweather was a right person" (146). Fairweather reassures alarmed Grenfell by promising to disappear at the end of the summer, when his work will be over and his portable house will depart to the South Seas (146). But Fairweather has a fatal flaw, at least from Grenfell's perspective: "He couldn't resist the appeal of ignorance. He had sensed in half an hour that this man loved the island. . . . In their talk Professor Fairweather had come to realize that this man had quite an unusual feeling for the island, therefore he would certainly like to know more about it—all he could tell him!" (148). Even in our amusement here, we notice how the pronouns blend two characters as they blended in section 4 of "The Bear." But that geologist with too much information to give still has one thing of uncontested value: his daughter. She's still created to please: "It was a pleasure to look at her, just as it is a pleasure to look at any comely creature who shows breeding, delicate preferences. She had lovely eyes, lovely skin, lovely manners. She listened closely when Grenfell and her father talked, but she didn't bark up with her opinions. . . . She answered him lightly, as if her impressions could matter only to herself, but, having an opinion, it was only good manners to admit it. 'Sweet, but decided,' was his rough estimate" (145–46). The daughter most definitely belongs to Fairweather.

So what advice or information does Professor Cather offer to sole proprietor William Faulkner, trusting him to hear it eventually? First, find what will please you—for example, plucky youth. Then acknowledge your own pleasure: "Plucky youth is more bracing than enduring age" (166). Stop fussing about Venus; she can take care of herself as she always has. But admit that plucky youth can be quintessentially female. That's why "She surely did look like a little pink clam in her white shell!" (166). Try to emulate that pleasing female: "She hadn't dodged. She had gone out, and she had come back. She would have a happy day" (165–66). Then share your joy: "He was walking fast down the winding trails. [There's been one winding trail in every Cather novel, somewhere.] Everything since he left the cabin had been reassuring, delightful [He has superseded St. Peter's glum prognosis of a future—to live without delight. He's found delight.]" (166). In fact, he's found delight where all delight must start: not in Yeats's foul rag-and-bone shop of the heart but in the raw heart nonetheless: "Everything was the same, and so was he! The air, or the smell of fir trees—something had sharpened his appetite. He was hungry." To be hungry is to feel like his best young self. So take and eat! "As he passed the grandfather tree he waved his hand, but didn't stop. . . . He crossed the sharp line from the deep shade to the sunny hillside behind his cabin and saw the wood smoke rising from the chimney." He smells the coffee. William knows to go ahead and "was wisely breakfasting" (166). So where does this leave the double, the shadow, the Catherian Henry? "As he came down the hill Grenfell was chuckling to himself." He has stopped worrying about that island, about who controls it, who uses it, who's the king of it. He gets ready to break fast.

In *The Reivers*, Faulkner signaled in five clear ways that he had followed this story, and planned to say the final word after he picked up the gage/glove or gauntlet. He has Lucius say lucidly,

> Secure behind that inviolable and inescapable rectitude concomitant with the name I bore, patterned on the knightly shapes of my male ancestors as bequeathed — nay, compelled — to me by my father's word-of-mouth, further bolstered and made vulnerable to shame by my mother's doting conviction, I had been merely testing Boon; not trying my own virtue but simply testing Boon's capacity to undermine it; and in my innocence, trusting too much in the armor and shield of innocence. . . .
>
> So Boon beat me in fair battle, using, as a gentleman should and would, gloves. (50–51)

The words *knightly, gentleman, armor and shield* make the *gloves* function as a *correction* to Cather's Shakespeare scholarship. For in *Richard II*, Bolingbroke and Mowbray throw *gages*. Faulkner gages his rival, as the dramatis personae do also. But, not to be mean-spirited about it, he also adds that all passengers who ride in the kind of car owned by Boss Priest wear "special costumes" that include "gauntlet gloves" (28–29).

First, he chooses that archaically spelled title to suggest that the following story will be about scavenging, which can include some old-fashioned and amusing prank-playing as well as some serious pillaging. The subtitle, "A Reminiscence," suggests "A Child's Reminiscence," an earlier title of "Out of the Cradle Endlessly Rocking," where Whitman's young boy learns what he is for, as Faulkner's young boy will learn he is for taking over the *reins*. Second, the novel's first words, in capital letters, are GRANDFATHER SAID: the book will primarily concern those kinds of grandfathers we have previously discussed in this book—the kind Lucius Priest can boast. Grandfathers are human, evil, long-lasting, powerful, knowledgeable, worth saluting. They're what the *race* depends on to move it forward. Third, almost immediately Faulkner inserts the phrase "time-honored Lancaster" (31), to finish echoing all that Myra-like murmuring about "Old John of Gaunt," which has led our memories to the *Henry IV* plays. He also describes that old Hell Creek trickster as "a *gaunt* man" (88, my italics), that is, one of a line of rascally kings. Fourth, since Cather had co-opted the eternal past by looking backward to the first frog-toad, Faulkner takes history and time forward by doubling the generational spread of the tale to eight generations. This story stretches by implication to the framing narrator's grandchildren and therefore into the beyond. The framing narrator who says GRANDFATHER SAID is the grandson of the plot's eleven-year-old Lucius Priest. Faulkner has doubled the fun and the stakes by adding the four-generation stories together. But he also—and repeatedly—uses analogies and jokes to jump out of the narrative present, our past, and into the publication present, the story's future (109, 110, 169, 193). Fifth, he takes Cather's advice—or shows her ghost what real comedy is—and in the process enjoys the telling, by the look of it. That is, he enjoys watching a plucky young person do a hard thing without balking, and makes us cheerfully acknowledge the feat with him. As we read in *Henry IV, Part 2*, "Well, thus we play the fools with the time, and the spirits of the wise sit in clouds and mock us" (2.2.154–56).

Since they've both been "ghosting along" for some time, Faulkner seems to make answering back to "Before Breakfast" as important as if Cather were still around to hear and understand. He lets her choose the weapons and the clearing, as dueling protocol requires, then accepts the Shakespearean allusion as their weapon of choice and fastens like a snapping turtle on *Henry IV*. He sees her three-play ploy and adopts it. He concentrates a good bit of his energy on material from *Henry IV, Part*

2, where Hal ends by gaining his crown, accepting himself, and growing up. Faulkner's Priest does these things in half the years it takes Shakespeare's Prince to do them. But the major characters come from *IV, Part 1*. Faulkner focuses his action through an eleven-year-old Yoknapatawphan Prince of Wales (wails?). Lucius is his light, as well as limb of Lucifer. And Lucius manages all he does as a prepubescent *boy* and grandson, not a daughter, as if that were part of the point, even in a gentleman's contest with an old lady. Faulkner uses Shakespeare's material to draw parallel characters, especially for Boon and Ned. While these three central characters derive from *Henry IV, Part 1*, much of the plot comes from *IV, Part 2*. *Richard II* contributes its first line, "Old John of Gaunt, time-honoured Lancaster," of course, but John of Gaunt points back to Edward, the first grandfather in the Shakespearean saga, whose seven sons establish more than one ruling line for the England of past and future. Faulkner identifies the real Shakespearean grandfather correctly as Edward. As his last stroke, he then dedicates his book to his grandchildren.

Faulkner starts with the young prince or Priest who chooses to consort with lowlife characters. Like birds of a feather, they flock to lowlife places while doing disreputable things. There's the huge man with every low appetite and no internal compunctions about satisfying any of them—Boon Hogganbeck, our Falstaff, at the beck and call of every illicit diversion. Boon is "the hulking giant" (26) who "was six feet four inches tall and weighed two hundred and forty pounds" (19). Then there's the Ned Poins of Faulkner's story, that Ned McCaslin who judges Boon a clown and contrives devices to "take a purse" while withholding respect, but not derision, from his ostensible superior. "Never did Ned let any of us forget that he . . . was an actual grandson to old time-honoured Lancaster" (31). The Prince Hal here, young Lucius Priest, keeps company with these social inferiors because he enjoys what they do, like any potential grandfather or future leader. He especially likes a double con, such as Shakespeare's encouraging robbery before robbing the robbers. A princely (or Priestly) young Hal plans to give the booty to the deserving—whether it be stolen purses or horses or automobiles, or money won by illicit betting at a racetrack, or even a gold tooth. Falstaff says to the prince, "We that take purses go by the moon and the seven stars" (*Part 1*, 1.2.15). The reivers' comic stroll through the Memphis streets with a stolen horse and a whore, late Sunday night, echoes "We have heard the chimes at midnight, Master Shallow" (*Part 2*, 2.4.603). Or, as Miss Reba summarizes the scene rhetorically, "A whore, a Pullman conductor and a Missippi swamp rat the size of a water tank leading a race horse through Memphis at midnight Sunday night, and nobody will notice it?" (136). Mistress Quickly's "quiet" tavern that features the amorous activities of Doll Tearsheet converts to Miss Reba's Catalpa Street "boarding house," where they keep the Sabbath decorously and carefully dole out the liquor.

Lucius is as good at "scraping his foot" or "making his manners" as courteous Hal is dependably ready to pay the bill. His disapproving father shares Henry IV's paternal dismay that "riot and dishonor stain the brow / Of my young Harry" (*Part 1*, 1.1.85). The prince, whether Hal or Lucius, is "the most comparative, rascaliest, sweet young prince" (*Part 1*, 1.2.91); and one point of picking up the allusion is for Faulkner to endorse Shakespeare's theme: that the rascaliest young prince can choose, when he is ready to end his misadventures, to remake himself into a trustworthy leader, eventual patriarch, and grandfather, who can teach a beloved grandson that a lad with the right stuff can become a fine king—or Priest. The path to such greatness may lead through seamy Memphis Eastcheaps, but one can still emerge to take a responsible place, as long as he doesn't forget what he's learned, doesn't break his pledges, and doesn't quit what he's started: "A gentleman accepts the responsibility of his actions and the burden of their consequences" (302).

Before such rebirth occurs in Shakespeare, Prince Hal's question is, "Where shall we take a purse tomorrow, Jack?" (*Part 1*, 1.2.111). Hal is more than ready for mischief, as Lucius also is instantly compliant and complicit. All Faulkner has to do is to translate highway robbery into betting on horse races, a weakness so destructive that Miss Reba evicts her pimp Mr. Binford every time he's caught doing it. Taking a purse may be Falstaff's vocation, but he recognizes Ned Poins as his superior in plotting or planning: "O, if men were to be saved by merit, what hole in hell were hot enough for him?" (*Part 1*, 1.2.119–20). In *The Reivers*, Ned (a nickname for *Edward*) McCaslin, after all, is the scamp nearest the source, the ur-grandfather, who'll do anything: old LCQ McCaslin. "Never did Ned let any of us forget that he . . . was an actual grandson to old time-honored Lancaster" (31). Whether in Faulkner or Shakespeare, a Ned serves as "the most omnipotent villain" (*Part 1*, 1.2.119). When they simply must win a particular heat, Ned tells Lucius, "Just before them judges and such hollers Go! you say to yourself *My name is Ned William McCaslin* and then do it." When Lucius asks, "Do what?" Ned replies, "I don't know yet neither" (263). The large man, whether Boon or Falstaff, "will give the devil his due" (*Part 1*, 1.2.132). He defers to Ned, his superior in chicanery. The parallels keep so close that Shakespeare's Falstaff makes the same jokes about Ned's breaking wind that Boon does, when Boon discovers Ned hiding in their borrowed car as a stowaway.

The grandfather theme rears its head like a snake even in Shakespeare's comic scenes. Falstaff says, "Indeed, I am not John of Gaunt, your grandfather; but yet no coward, Hal" (*Part 1*, 2.2.70–71). And Hal, like Lucius, says of himself, "Though I be Prince of Wales, yet I am the King of courtesy . . . a lad of mettle, a good boy (*Part 1*, 2.4.11, 13–14). In short, both parts of *Henry IV* quickly supply Faulkner with material for his comic romp to prove that the rascaliest young scamp, if gently bred, can grow up to be a wise and understanding grandfather, especially if he has four such grandfathers in his background to show him the way, as Lucius had and as Hal, soon to be Henry V, did.

Henry IV, Part 2 provides a great deal of fodder for Faulkner's horse race. Its prologue is started by "Rumour, painted full of tongues." Rumor passes as quickly from one tongue to another in England as in Parsham, Tennessee, where word of an unofficial, illicit horse race draws a dependable crowd. Rumor helps events move quickly. In England,

> Every minute now
> should be the father to some stratagem.
> The times are wild. Contention, like a horse
> full of high feeding, madly hath broke loose
> And bears down all before him.
>   (*Part 2*, 1.1.9–11)

And in Tennessee, "All it took for a horse race was two horses with the time to run a race, within ten miles of each other, and the air itself spread the news of it" (217). At the play's end, the king confesses "by what bypaths and indirect crooked ways / I met this crown" (*Part 2*, 4.5.185–86). In the middle, we see the representatives of the state betray and entrap their opponents. As Faulkner reminds us, "Fortune is a fickle jade" (48), for a jade is a tired horse.

Part 2 supplies Faulkner a Shakespearean model for his brothel scenes. Either writer requires two dramatized women, one "seasoned" (Mistress Quickly, Miss Reba), one young (Doll Tearsheet, Everbe Corinthia). The scene exploits the comedy of the big man's frustrated desire to bed the young woman. It includes careful watching done by the young prince/priest. Both the young heir and the corrupt older Ned disguise themselves as menials or apprentices, and watch Boon or Falstaff brag and bray. Brawling ensues in both places, to which the proprietress strenuously objects. In both scenes we recognize the aptness of the line "How subject we old men are to the vice of lying!" (3.2.325). *Part 2* also contributes other important ingredients to *The Reivers*. There's swaggering Pistol, "the foul mouth'st rogue in England" (2.2.596), instantly disliked and rejected by the women. Pistol, the overbearing Shakespeare buffoon, equates to Deputy Sheriff Butch from Hardwick. As the first Shakespearean frontispiece features Pistol, Faulkner chooses to start his novel with a pistol scene, in which Boon jumps into the livery stable scrambling for a pistol with which to shoot Ludus: feature accounted for. Then there's Shakespeare's honest and dependable Chief Justice, who has the integrity to jail Prince Hal when justice requires and is rewarded for virtue and valor. In Faulkner, Constable Poleymus (*polymerus* means "having many parts") has the courage to confront pistol-toting Butch, to jail Boon, and to hire Corrie to care for his helpless wife. Ned's fourth-heat betrayal of his allies by betting against his own horse and failing to make him run, thus entrapping others in one more devious trick, also has a parallel in Shakespeare: Prince John entraps and executes disloyal Northumberland and Mowbray while sticking disingenuously (they feel dishonorably) to the letter of the law and the literal word. Finally, both Shakespeare's and Faulkner's actions end with tearful confrontations between fathers (or grandfathers) and sons; each son then resolves to bear his responsibilities like a man and to keep apart from the big man. Lucius approaches Boon's new abode only a year later, to see Boon's legitimate newborn son, named Lucius Priest Hogganbeck. The name is Faulkner's near-perfect farewell symbol for doubleness, his final summary accepting double possibilities for almost everything.

Faulkner cares in this novel to designate what it takes to build successfully the characters of the kings (or High Priests) to be, the plucky youth of the future. Perhaps he wishes to pass along to them the kind of wisdom Cather transferred to him. He underscores the opportunity to sin, as well as the audacity to seize that opportunity: there'll be no Hadleyburg mistakes either for Shakespeare or for Faulkner here. Both adopt the "Lead Us into Temptation" approach. Both acknowledge that to "banish plump Jack . . . [means you] banish all the world" (*Part 1*, 2.4.527). One will need a quick brain to learn survival skills in any place (whether in the knife-fights of a whorehouse attic or in sleeping to wake with Uncle Parsham in his black aristocrat's cabin). One will need a good ear to hear sound advice from wicked experts such as Ned, or to notice the implications when he gives none. One will need good manners and humility before Boss Priest and one's superiors.

One also needs a faith that reform can extend to others, as well as oneself. Lucius believes in Everbe's resolves as well as his own. He can thus forgive her occasional slippage, just as if he were Bolingbroke or Hal. He seems to tell his own grandsons that no person can avoid falling into grievous error, but anyone can admit straightforwardly what has been done, without making excuses. Then man or woman can remember what he or she has seen and learned while doing it. That makes a forgiven sinner the opposite of Boon, as Prince Hal is opposite Falstaff, because Falstaff, like Boon, illustrates "the disease of not listening, and not marking" (*Part 2*, 1.2.137–40). Educable heirs, like Prince Hal or Lucius, can be awed by enemies, as Hal is of Hotspur, without being afraid to face and fight them, as Lucius is not afraid of Otis or experienced McWillie.

The combat in Shakespeare is as full of thundering hooves as Hightower's daydreams. It is to be "as full of spirit as the month of May / And gorgeous as the sun at midsummer" (*Part 1*, 4.1.101–2). Hotspur, the awesome opponent, looks confidently to "my horse / who is to bear me like a thunderbolt" (4.1.119–20). Eschewing the grossly obvious, our horse-borrowers name their entry not Thunderbolt, but Lightning. For their last race, however, "McWillie and I crouched our poised thunderbolts" (272). They also willingly anticipate the equivalent moment when "Harry to

Harry shall, hot horse to horse, meet" (122–23). Once Faulkner's deliberate parallels are firmly established, he can exploit such Shakespearean lines as "Go, . . . [Ned], to horse, to horse" (*Part 1*, 3.3.220). The slim difference among these battlers and brigands appears in the ostensible codes they carry into their contests. Falstaff famously renounces honor (*Part 1*, 5.1) and stays free of injury; Boon, incapable of Falstaff's cool strategy near battle, is jailed for assault and misses the heroic moment.

Faulkner, as Cather, valorizes his own sex as the hope of the future. Hence, these hopes lie in somewhat different qualities or responses. The geologist's daughter who doesn't dodge the cold waves in "Before Breakfast" swims alone and keeps her pledge to herself. Faulkner's Young Priest will always race in front of judgmental spectators. Those who watch will bet on the outcome. He can't assume his allies and friends—his Boons or Neds or Miss Rebas—will put their money on the horse he rides. He's alone in this crowd. Lucius explains, "I was alone. . . . I was anything but solitary. I was an island in that ring of sweated hats" (244). But proprietor of his island self, he can still run the race and finish the course and keep faith with his promises. And he can still remain convincing while his creator writes what seems to me, hands down and no quibbling, the greatest horse race ever penned on paper.

In both final statements, or in their last constructed fictions, our two great American writers take an unblinking look around them and then acknowledge—in words—the best and worst they see. The worst is always a part of themselves. Yet they confidently decide that young folks will swim or ride out dangerously, and then come back dependably, because they can do it. They will have a happy day. In both North and South, we foresee happy days. The writers agree that both of them have run races, from time to time, in which they had hidden advantages. Some legal conservatives would call these contests fixed, unfair. But they were still good enough to run, and even good enough to run against each other. So they showed they really knew their tricks; they proved themselves winners of the kind made by a blend of rascally knave and grandparent. Finally, in their last fictions, they played the other's hand: Cather rooted a man on his own little postage stamp, and Faulkner described cross-country movement so swift that he set a new standard. They turned and bet on each other. In that last moment, that last tricky reversal, Cather memorialized a man who loved his blessed isolation because it preserved his kind of order. Faulkner, conversely, lifted up a race toward the open stretch into the future. They not only changed horses in midstream; they swapped with each other.

Many times in his last twenty years, Faulkner talked of breaking his pencil. After he had used it on *The Reivers*, he almost seemed for a moment to change characters. He went docilely and civilly to West Point and behaved well there, as Blotner relates with a hint of surprise. Of course, the military academy was at that moment headed by Westmoreland, also a name in *Henry IV, Part 2*. It couldn't have hurt this visit that Shakespeare's Westmoreland was on King Henry's side. After Faulkner finished *The Reivers*, he started drinking heavily as was his custom. The book was published June 4. Meanwhile, Faulkner was in Oxford when he fell from his horse, injured himself painfully, and was committed in great pain to his customary sanitarium in Byhalia on July 5. He died suddenly on July 6, mission accomplished.

NOTES

INTRODUCTION

1. Urgo, *Cather and the Myth*, 107–8. While the essential argument of this book is contained in these two pages, Urgo's phrase for it was used in a printed interview about the book, with Karl Rosenquist as interviewer, published in *wcpmn&r* 61, no. 1 (1997): 16–21.

2. The two-volume *The World and the Parish* contains dozens, perhaps hundreds, of Cather's reviews of her contemporary writers as well as performing artists. For her reading of romantics and modernists, see Rosowski and Middleton.

3. Skaggs, "Willa Cather and the Father of History"; see also Williams.

4. See "My First Novels (There Were Two)," in *Cather on Writing*, 89–98.

5. The first list of such references was in Wittenberg's "Faulkner and Women Writers."

1. A STARTING POINT

1. "In a letter to Ferris Greenslet dated January 21, 1928, Cather said she would not comment in print on another writer's book. . . . She proclaimed in a letter of February 6, 1930, that she would never comment on a living writer's work" (Chinn, 72 n. 7).

2. Blotner says Faulkner's eyes were hazel (1:211) while Cather says they were blue.

3. Cather's "painted ships" analogy may be designed to suggest Homeric epics, artful and idealized designs, or the narrative "constructions"

of official history. What Faulkner picked up here is *Homer*. He uses the name throughout his early published pieces. In "A Rose for Emily," for example, he features Homer Barron—clearly a resonating name.

2. BUZZING

1. This cover is replicated in Roorda's "Cather in the Magazines."

2. I cannot help wondering whether Faulkner is hinting through this name his accurate perception that Cather paints in Henry James's colors as she wanders toward Oz.

3. See Skaggs, "Cather's Great Emersonian Environmental Quartet," 199–200.

4. Cather may get her association with Augusta from a Henry James character in *Roderick Hudson* named Augusta Blanchard, who paints pale watercolors.

5. Cather, *OB* 162. According to James Woodress, "Before Breakfast" was written during the summer of 1944, "but the effort was costly" (498). It was published in this posthumous volume in the year following Cather's death on April 24, 1947.

6. *Go Down, Moses* may have triggered Cather's writing the story. It answers her last novel, *Sapphira and the Slave Girl*, as we shall see.

7. The overtone divined but not heard is suggested, of course, in the essay "The Novel Démeublé."

8. Cather used the line to describe the sentiments of her own first published essay on Carlyle, placed without her knowledge in the Lincoln *Journal*. She said the bitter feelings were roused in her by a fervid reading of Carlyle (Woodress 72–73).

3. POSSESSION

1. For further information on Viola Roseboro' see Skaggs, "Viola Roseboro': A Prototype."

2. According to Susan Snell, "When the house burned, the Stones lost not only Faulkner poetry manuscripts, but also, as they listed in an insurance inventory, files for 'numbers of years' of *Poetry*, the *New Republic*, the *Double Dealer*, as well as 'others now quite rare'" (72).

3. Amanda (Brooke) Ethridge presented this and other basic facts concerning Faulkner and Tom Outland at the Tenth International Cather Seminar, Red Cloud and Lincoln NE, June 18–25, 2005.

4. The three peaks of those buttes, however, are oddly reminiscent of the three mountain peaks mentioned on Ahab's coin in *Moby Dick*. The odd chance-choice-design theme Cather develops is also, as we have mentioned, reminiscent of Queequeg's loom theme, mentioned in the last chapter. Faulkner's love of *Moby Dick* is well known.

4. THE SOUNDS BECOME FURY

1. The novel was featured in Nebraska's "One Book, One State" reading campaign in 2005, after Chicago initiated the idea by hailing it as the book the whole city was reading in 2003. Oprah sold millions of Faulkner books through her Faulkner summer of 2005.

2. Susan Snell, author of *Phil Stone of Oxford*, kindly wrote me in 1992, "Stone's book orders at New Haven's Brick Row, a year when he/they seemed to be buying all current serious fiction, does include a request for Cather's *My Ántonia* in June, 1922."

3. As far as I know, Joseph R. Urgo was first to suggest this fact in a paper he read for the Faulkner section of the ALA annual meeting: "Sense of History and Place: Willa Cather and William Faulkner," American Literature Association, San Diego CA, June 1994.

4. Sarah Gardam presented a paper entitled "Subverting the Male Gaze: Willa Cather's Lena Lingard and William Faulkner's Lena Grove" at the Tenth International Cather Seminar, Red Cloud and Lincoln NE, June 19, 2005. The paper is included in the forthcoming volume of the conference's best essays, *Violence, the Arts, and Cather*, edited by Urgo and Skaggs.

5. For a full explanation of this technique, see Skaggs, "Cather's Radical Empiricism."

6. My neighbor James Morgan recently handed me a photograph of the street renamed "Pirate's Alley," in New Orleans, where Faulkner once lived. It features a streetlight with a lantern shape.

7. Joseph R. Urgo reminded me of this fact when generously reading an early version of this manuscript.

8. Triangles are also central features in such other Cather works as *The Professor's House*, *My Mortal Enemy*, *Sapphira and the Slave Girl*, "Old Mrs. Harris," "Two Friends," and "Neighbour Rosicky." In all, she triangulates.

9. Faulkner "urged moderation, saying that just as he opposed forced segregation, he opposed forced integration" (Parini 383).

10. The statement appeared in the *Reporter* of March 22, 1956.

11. The works I am referencing here are two unpublished essays: Goodman, "William Faulkner's Probable Debt"; and Middleton, "Cather, Faulkner, and the Family of Man."

5. DUST TRACKS ON SOME ROADS

1. *New York Times*, June 28, 2005, Arts sec., pp. 1, 7.

2. See two of my essays: "A Good Girl in Her Place" and "Cather's Use of Parkman's Histories."

3. Faulkner scholar James Carothers pointed out this short story to me at the Faulkner Conference in Oxford, Mississippi, in July 2002.

4. Nancy Sherwood, of the wcpm staff, e-mailed me on August 23, 2005, "concerning the Farmer's and Merchant's Bank. Construction began in 1888 and [it] opened in June 1889. Directors included Silas Garber, President; George Holland, Vice President; W. S. Garber, Cashier. . . . Correspondents were Kountz Bros., New York; First National Bank, Omaha; First National Bank, Lincoln."

5. *Singleton* is the name of Henry James's only heroic artist, in his novel *Roderick Hudson*. He is once compared cynically to an insect, because of his unremitting work. I have argued elsewhere (in "Cather's Violent Appropriations") that this novel is one of the *most* important of Cather's literary influences, and that references to it are pervasive in her work.

6. SPARRING

1. Adams's collection was the first contribution to the Caspersen Cather Collection at Drew University. These contrasting papers were presented at a colloquium celebrating that collection, September 30–October 1, 2005. They are slated for publication in a volume collecting the colloquium presentations, entitled *Willa Cather: New Facts, New Glimpses, Revisions*, ed. John J. Murphy and Merrill M. Skaggs (Madison nj: Fairleigh Dickinson University Press, forthcoming).

2. Woodress 438. The anthology was edited by Whit Burnett and was called *This Is My Best*.

3. I'd class such works as *My Ántonia*, *The Professor's House*, "Old Mrs.

Harris," and *Sapphira and the Slave Girl* as tours de force that she makes "autobiographical" expressly in order to reinforce her own authority in executing extravagantly complex tasks that make her nervous about eventual success. I think she brings them all off.

4. Jessica Rabin explores the connections between Jewish Rosens and Christian rose windows in "Like a Rose among Thorns."

7. TIT FOR TAT

1. Tenth International Cather Seminar: "Violence, the Arts, and Cather," Red Cloud and Lincoln NE, June 18–25, 2005; plenary speech, June 23. The paper will be included in the forthcoming volume *Violence, the Arts, and Cather*, ed. Urgo and Skaggs.

2. I'm very grateful to Janis Stout for tracking down this hard-to-find article in the *Literary Review of the New York Evening Post* for Saturday, Nov. 4, 1922. A photocopy of it can be found in the Caspersen Cather Collection at Drew University.

3. David Massey, who wrote the first Cather dissertation in Drew's Caspersen School of Graduate Studies, examined the significant juxta-positions in *Song of the Lark*.

4. This motif was first brought to my attention in an essay by Patricia Sell entitled "Marian Forrester's 'Fine Play-Acting,'" at that point sub-mitted to the WCPMN&R. Also at that time I commented in a reader's report that a larger thesis might expand to show "that the acting Mar-ian Forrester clearly does in *A Lost Lady* fits a pattern of theatrical ref-erences emerging in *every* Cather novel, when one looks for them: the contrasting 'performances' of Winifred and Hilda in *Alexander's Bridge*; the lecture on drama, art, religion, and mystery in *The Professor's House*; the miracle play motif in *Shadows on the Rock*; the costs of performance theme in *The Song of the Lark* and *Lucy Gayheart*, Myra Henshawe's 'theatrics' in *My Mortal Enemy*, just for starters."

5. For the record, I suspect that this reference to Boeotian ignorance, like the references to *Henry IV*, originate in Mark Twain's work, the first in his "How to Tell a Story" and the second in his "1601."

8. LITERARY HOPSCOTCH

1. Cather's *most* male-centered world is developed in *The Professor's House*. But even in that exceptional novel, one finds a relatively complex

wife, two daughters, threatening female neighbor, and central symbol: Mother Eve. *Death Comes for the Archbishop* includes two male protagonists, but its only important female, Cather joked, is the Virgin Mary, not to mention the Church Herself (Woodress 396; Stout, *Calendar*, no. 890).

2. For the competitive relationship between these two women, both of whose names Faulkner invoked when asked about women writers, see my "Interlocking Works."

3. She represents many of the traits Faulkner first depicted in "A Rose for Emily," and even memorialized in his protagonist Emily Grierson, with Ellen Glasgow's initials.

4. I trace this type in *Folk of Southern Fiction*.

5. This announcement was part of her plenary address at the Cather seminar producing the collection of essays edited by Ann Romines and entitled *Willa Cather's Southern Connections*.

6. Urgo splendidly orchestrates this motif in "'Dock Burs in Yo' Pants.'"

7. The phrase resonates partially because it occurs in *Death Comes for the Archbishop* as cardinals "watch the evening come on" (13), or in Faulkner's longer version of the story title "That Evening Sun Go Down." The twilight has seemed especially important to both.

9. CROSSING THE FINISH LINES

1. See my essay in the forthcoming volume covering the "Willa Cather as Cultural Icon" conference held in Breadloaf, Vermont, in 2003. I argue in this essay that Cather satirized Kate Chopin, Edith Wharton, and Ellen Glasgow in "The Old Beauty," the title story; in "The Best Years," she acknowledges her whole writing life by including one detail matching a corresponding item from each of her own novels, plus her three stories of *Obscure Destinies*. Then, having surveyed her career, Cather centers that story around a young sister who is eager to "go home." Having written "The Best Years" as her last story, Cather died. The conference's collection of essays is slated to be published by the University of Nebraska Press.

2. Dennis Coyle also believes that *Margaret*, the name of Grenfell's wife, references Margaret Powers from *Soldier's Pay* as well as the wife of

Henry VI, thereby extending the Shakespearean allusion to more Henrys. See the forthcoming (Winter 2007) issue of *WCPMN&R*.

3. *Richard II* 3.2.11. All quotations of Shakespeare's plays are from the *Complete Works*, Kittredge ed.; references are to act, scene, and line.

4. Marvin Friedman has traced the connection between "Before Breakfast" and *My Mortal Enemy* in his "Lifting the Death Chill."

5. I'm fascinated that these two avid miners of Mark Twain—Cather and Faulkner—will share Twain's backhanded tribute to Shakespeare's *Henry IV*, which Twain drops into "1601." That frisky romp in Shakespeare's England, which some consider pornographic, is built around the implicit metaphor of constipation and digestion, that is, of farts and old farts. There's an analogy here to Grenfell's stomach.

6. This slightly misquoted line subtly suggests that a Myra-type narcissist needs to brush up her Shakespeare.

WORKS CITED

Beer, Thomas. "Miss Cather." *The Borzoi*. New York: Knopf, 1925.

Caspersen Cather Collection, Drew University, Madison NJ.

Blotner, Joseph. *Faulkner: A Biography*. 2 vols. New York: Random, 1974.

———. *Faulkner: A Biography*. New York: Random, 1984.

Callander, Marilyn Berg. *Willa Cather and the Fairy Tale*. Ann Arbor: University of Michigan Research Press, 1989.

Cather, Willa. *Death Comes for the Archbishop*. New York: Vintage Books, 1971.

———. "The House on Charles Street." *Literary Review of the New York Evening Post* 3, no. 9 (Nov. 4, 1922): 173–74.

———. *A Lost Lady*. New York: Knopf, 1923.

———. *Lucy Gayheart*. New York: Knopf, 1935.

———. *My Ántonia*. Sentry Edition. Boston: Houghton Mifflin, 1918.

———. *My Mortal Enemy*. New York: Knopf, 1926.

———. *Not Under Forty*. Lincoln: University of Nebraska Press, 1988.

———. *O Pioneers!* Boston: Houghton Mifflin, 1941.

———. *The Old Beauty*. New York: Knopf, 1948.

———. *One of Ours*. New York: Vintage Books, 1950.

———. *The Professor's House*. New York: Knopf, 1925.

———. *Sapphira and the Slave Girl*. New York: Knopf, 1940.

———. *Shadows on the Rock*. New York: Knopf, 1931.

———. *The Song of the Lark*. Lincoln: University of Nebraska Press, 1978.

———. *The Song of the Lark*. Ed. Sherrill Harbison. New York: Penguin, 1999.

———. *Willa Cather on Writing: Critical Studies on Writing as an Art*. Lincoln: University of Nebraska Press, 1988.

———. *The World and the Parish: Willa Cather's Articles and Reviews, 1893–1902*. Ed. William M. Curtin. Lincoln: University of Nebraska Press, 1970.

Chinn, Nancy. "'My Six Books Would Be': The Cather-Hurston Connection." *WCPMN&R* 45, no. 3 (2002): 72, n. 7.

Cowley, Malcolm. *The Faulkner-Cowley File: Letters and Memories, 1944–62*. New York: Viking, 1966.

Cox, Dianne L., ed. *William Faulkner's As I Lay Dying: A Critical Casebook*. New York: Garland, 1985.

Coyle, Dennis. "A Farewell: Faulkner and Allusions to Shakespeare in Willa Cather's 'Before Breakfast.'" *WCPMN&R* 50, no. 3 (Winter, 2007) 60–62.

Early, James. *The Making of Go Down, Moses*. Dallas: Southern Methodist University Press, 1972.

Etheridge, Amanda. "Phil Stone and Tom Outland." Paper presented at the Tenth International Cather Seminar. Red Cloud and Lincoln NE, June 18–25, 2005.

Fant, Joseph L., III, and Robert Ashley, eds. *Faulkner at West Point*. New York: Random, 1964.

Faulkner, William. *Absalom, Absalom!* New York: Modern Library, 1964.

———. *As I Lay Dying: The Corrected Text*. New York: Vintage International, 1985.

———. *Go Down, Moses*. 1942; New York: Vintage International, 1990.

———. *Light in August*. Introduction by Cleanth Brooks. New York: Modern Library, 1968.

———. *The Marble Faun and A Green Bough*. New York: Random House, 1960.

———. *Mosquitoes*. New York: Washington Square Press, 1985.

———. *New Orleans Sketches*. Ed. Carvel Collins. Jackson: University Press of Mississippi, 1958.

———. *The Reivers*. New York: Random, 1962.

———. *Sanctuary*. New York: Vintage Books, 1958.

———. *Sartoris*. New York: New American Library, 1964.

———. *Selected Letters of William Faulkner*. Ed. Joseph Blotner. New York: Vintage, 1978.

———. *Soldier's Pay*. New York: Liveright, 1954.

———. *The Sound and the Fury: The Corrected Text*. New York: Vintage International, 1990.

Friedman, Marvin. "Lifting the Death Chill: 'Before Breakfast' as Sequel to *My Mortal Enemy*." *WCPMN&R* 44, no. 3 (Winter/Spring 2002): 61–67.

Gardam, Sarah. "Subverting the Male Gaze: Willa Cather's Lena Lingard and William Faulkner's Lena Grove." In Urgo and Skaggs, *Violence, the Arts, and Cather* (forthcoming).

Godden, Richard, and Noel Polk, "Reading the Ledgers." *Mississippi Quarterly* 55 (Fall 2003): 301–59.

Goodman, Charlotte. "William Faulkner's Probable Debt to Willa Cather: *A Lost Lady* and *The Sound and the Fury*." Paper presented at the annual meeting of the Northeast Modern Language Association, Wilmington DE, 1989.

Gwynn, Frederick L., and Joseph Blotner, eds. *Faulkner in the University: Class Conferences at the University of Virginia, 1957–1958*. Charlottesville: University of Virginia Press, 1980.

Hamblin, Robert W., and Charles A. Peek, eds. *A William Faulkner Encyclopedia*. Westport CT: Greenwood, 1999.

Harrell, David. *From Mesa Verde to The Professor's House*. Albuquerque: University of New Mexico Press, 1990.

Irving, John. Interview. *New York Times*, June 28, 2005. Arts sec.

Johnston, Richard Malcolm. "Mr. Joseph Pate and His People." In *The Primes and Their Neighbors: Ten Tales of Middle Georgia*. New York: Appleton, 1891.

Kartiganer, Donald. *The Fragile Thread: The Meaning of Form in Faulkner's Novels*. Amherst: University of Massachusetts Press, 1979.

———. "In Place of an Introduction: Reading Faulkner." In *Faulkner at 100: Retrospect and Prospect*, ed. Donald M. Kartiganer and Ann J. Abadie, xiv–xx. Jackson: University Press of Mississippi, 2000.

Kittredge, George Lymon, ed. *The Complete Works of Shakespeare*. Boston: Ginn, 1936.

Kreiswirth, Martin. *William Faulkner: The Making of a Novelist*. Athens: University of Georgia Press, 1983.

Kvasnicka, Mellanee. "Education in the Parish: Preparation for the World." *WCPMN&R* 43, no. 3 (2000): 64.

Lewis, Edith. *Willa Cather Living: A Personal Record*. New York: Knopf, 1953.

Meriwether, James B., and Michael Millgate, eds. *Lion in the Garden: Interviews with William Faulkner, 1926–1962*. New York: Random House, 1968.

Middleton, Jo Ann. "Cather, Faulkner, and The Family of Man: or, How Did He Ever Think Up the Compsons?" Paper presented at the annual meeting of the American Literature Association, San Diego, 1994.

———. *Willa Cather's Modernism: A Study of Style and Technique*. Madison NJ: Fairleigh Dickinson University Press, 1990.

Minter, David. *William Faulkner: His Life and Work*. Baltimore: Johns Hopkins University Press, 1980.

Nestrick, William V. "The Function of Form in 'The Bear, Section IV.'" *Twentieth Century Literature* 12, no. 3 (Oct. 1966): 131–37.

Oates, Stephen B. *Faulkner: The Man and the Artist*. New York: Harper, 1987.

Parini, Jay. *One Matchless Time: A Life of William Faulkner*. New York: Harper, 2004.

Peek, Charles A. "*As I Lay Dying*." In Hamblin and Peek 20–23.

Porter, David. "Cather on Cather II: Two Recent Acquisitions at Drew University." *WCPMN&R* 46, no. 3 (Winter–Spring 2003): 49, 53–58.

Rabin, Jessica. "Like a Rose among Thorns: Ethnicity, Demography, and Otherness in Willa Cather's 'Old Mrs. Harris.'" In *Willa Cather's New York*, ed. Merrill Maguire Skaggs, 266–78. Madison NJ: Fairleigh Dickinson University Press, 2000.

Romines, Ann, ed. *Willa Cather's Southern Connections*. Charlottesville: University of Virginia Press, 2000.

Roorda, Rebecca. "Willa Cather in the Magazines: The Business of Art." *WCPMN&R* 44, no. 3 (Winter–Spring 2001): 71–75.

Rosowski, Susan J. *The Voyage Perilous: Willa Cather's Romanticism*. Lincoln: University of Nebraska Press, 1986.

Saavedra, Miguel de Cervantes. *Don Quixote, the Ingenious Gentleman of La Mancha*. Trans. John Ormsby. New York: Heritage, 1950.

Sensibar, Judith. *The Origins of Faulkner's Art.* Austin: University of Texas Press, 1984.

Sell, Patricia. "Marian Forrester's 'Fine Play Acting.'" Unpublished paper.

Skaggs, Merrill Maguire. "Cather's Complex Tale of a Simple Man: 'Neighbour Rosicky.'" In *Willa Cather: Family, Community, and History (The BYU Symposium)*, ed. John J. Murphy, 79–84. Provo UT: Brigham Young University Press, 1990.

——. "Cather's Use of Parkman's Histories in *Shadows on the Rock.*" In *Cather Studies II*, ed. Susan J. Rosowski, 140–55. Lincoln: University of Nebraska Press, 1993.

——. "Cather's Violent Appropriation of Henry James's Art." In Urgo and Skaggs, *Violence, the Arts, and Cather* (forthcoming).

——. "*Death Comes for the Archbishop*: Willa Cather's Varieties of Religious Experience." In *Willa Cather and the Culture of Belief*, ed. John J. Murphy, 101–22. Provo UT: Brigham Young University Press, 2002.

——. *The Folk of Southern Fiction.* Athens: University of Georgia Press, 1972.

——. "A Good Girl in Her Place: Cather's *Shadows on the Rock.*" *Religion and Literature* 17, no. 3 (Autumn 1985): 27–36.

——. "Icons and Willa Cather." In *Willa Cather as Cultural Icon*, ed. Guy Reynolds. Lincoln: University of Nebraska Press, 2007.

——. "The Interlocking Works of Willa Cather and Ellen Glasgow." In *Willa Cather's Southern Connections: New Essays on Cather and the South*, 158–69. Charlottesville: University Press of Virginia, 2000.

——. "Teaching 'Old Mrs. Harris.'" *Nebraska English Journal* 37 (Fall 1991): 75–84.

——. "Viola Roseboro': A Prototype for Cather's *My Mortal Enemy.*" *Mississippi Quarterly* 54, no. 1 (Winter 2000–2001): 5–22.

——. "Willa Cather and the Father of History: Mark Twain." In *Willa Cather and the American Southwest*, ed. John N. Swift and Joseph R. Urgo, 80–88. Lincoln: University of Nebraska Press, 2002.

——. "Willa Cather's Great Emersonian Environmental Quartet." In *Cather Studies 5*, ed. Susan J. Rosowski, 199–215. Lincoln: University of Nebraska Press, 2003.

——. "Willa Cather's Radical Empiricism." *WCPMN&R* 47, no. 1 (Summer 2003): 15–19.

Snell, Susan. *Phil Stone of Oxford: A Vicarious Life*. Athens: University of Georgia Press, 1991.

Stout, Janis P. *Willa Cather: The Writer and Her World*. Charlottesville: University of Virginia Press, 2000.

———, ed. *A Calendar of the Letters of Willa Cather*. Lincoln: University of Nebraska Press, 2002.

Svendsen, Kathleen Schairer. "Faulkner's 'Anse'-wer to Cather's Sick Rose: Anse Bundren as a Caricature of Anton Rosicky." *WCPMN&R* 50, no. 3 (Winter, 2007), 63–66.

Urgo, Joseph R. "'Dock Burs in Yo' Pants': Reading Cather through Sapphira and the Slave Girl." In Romines 24–37.

———. *Willa Cather and the Myth of American Migration*. Urbana: University of Illinois Press, 1995.

———, and Merrill Maguire Skaggs, eds. *Violence, the Arts, and Cather*. Madison NJ: Fairleigh Dickinson University Press, 2007.

Williams, Deborah Lindsay. "Pernicious Contact: Willa Cather and the Problem of Literary Sisterhood." In *Willa Cather's New York: New Essays on Cather in the City*, ed. Merrill Maguire Skaggs 211–22. Madison NJ: Fairleigh Dickinson University Press, 2000.

Williamson, Joel. *William Faulkner and Southern History*. Oxford: Oxford University Press, 1993.

Wittenberg, Judith. "Faulkner and Women Writers." In *Faulkner and Women*, ed. Doreen Fowler and Ann J. Abadie, 287–93. Jackson: University Press of Mississippi, 1986.

Woodress, James. *Willa Cather: A Literary Life*. Lincoln: University of Nebraska Press, 1987.

INDEX